Praise for The Morning After

"A persuasive critique . . . Katie Roiphe's brave book will be both heralded and condemned for its angry attack on 'rape crisis feminism.' . . . Roiphe doesn't have the answer . . . but at least she has the nerve to raise the question."
— *New York Times Book Review*

"A brilliant young contrarian voice, à la Mary McCarthy."
— *Kirkus*

"A prominent — and provocative — new voice in feminist debate."
— *New York Sunday Newsday*

"Katie Roiphe writes from the trenches of gender warfare. *The Morning After* is clearheaded, wry, disturbing."
— *Washington Post Book World*

"Remarkable — the first intelligent cry of protest from Roiphe's generation against what feminism has wrought in the name of woman."
— *Commentary*

The
Morning
After

The
Morning
After

Sex, Fear, and Feminism

Katie Roiphe

Little, Brown and Company

Boston   New York   Toronto   London

FIRST PAPERBACK EDITION

The names and circumstances of some people in this book have been modified for reasons of privacy.

"The Rape Crisis, or 'Is Dating Dangerous?' " has previously appeared in the *New York Times Magazine*.

Excerpt from "Chaos in Motion and Not in Motion" from *Collected Poems* by Wallace Stevens. © 1947 by Wallace Stevens. Reprinted by permission of Alfred A. Knopf, Inc.
 Excerpt from "Lullaby" from *Collected Poems* by W. H. Auden, edited by Edward Mendelson. © 1976, 1991 by the Estate of W. H. Auden. Reprinted by permission of Faber and Faber Ltd.
 Excerpt from "First Fig" from *Collected Poems* by Edna St. Vincent Millay, HarperCollins. © 1922, 1950 by Edna St. Vincent Millay. Reprinted by permission of Elizabeth Barnett, literary executor.

Library of Congress Cataloging-in-Publication Data
Roiphe, Katie.
   The morning after : sex, fear, and feminism /
by Katie Roiphe.
         p.   cm.
   ISBN 0-316-75431-5 (hc)
   ISBN 0-316-75432-3 (pb)
   1. Feminism and education—United States.   2. Education, Higher—
Political aspects—United States.   3. Feminism—United States.
4. Sexual harassment—United States.   I. Title.
LC197.R65   1993
370.19'345—dc20   93-18783

10 9 8 7 6 5 4 3 2 1

RRD-VA

Published simultaneously in Canada
by Little, Brown & Company (Canada) Limited

PRINTED IN THE UNITED STATES OF AMERICA

To Anne and Herman Roiphe,
always my first readers

Certainty, fidelity
On the stroke of midnight pass
Like vibrations of a bell,
And fashionable madmen raise
Their pedantic boring cry:
Every farthing of the cost,
All the dreaded cards foretell,
Shall be paid, but from this night
Not a whisper, not a thought,
Not a kiss nor look be lost.

—W. H. Auden

Contents

Acknowledgments

A lthough of course all responsibility for the content of this book falls on my own shoulders, and it reflects no one's opinions but my own, there are lots of people who have given me invaluable help. Thanks to Neil Gilbert, Catherine Stimpson, and all of the people, too numerous to mention, who told me what they thought. Thanks also to Ethel Person for first encouraging me to put my thoughts down on paper. I am grateful to my professors at Princeton University for their support, and for all they have taught me about literature, which inevitably filters into my writing, even on so different a subject.

I am greatly indebted to my agent, Suzanne Gluck, for her amazing energy and enthusiasm. This book has also benefited immeasurably from the careful attentions of my skillful editors, Jim Silberman and Jordan Pavlin.

I owe thanks to my friends and family who have lent ideas over the years and furnished this book with their stories and opinions. Thanks especially to Misha Glouberman

for our hours of analysis in college and to my sister Emily
Roiphe for her flashes of insight. I am grateful to Richard
Kaye for his loyalty and wit in adverse circumstances, and
to Josh Pashman for our endless and fruitful conversations.

Thanks also to my sister Becky Roiphe for her endur-
ing faith in me, her perspective, her advice, and most of all
for our sustaining daily phone calls. Finally I am grateful to
David Samuels for his nearly infinite patience and for the
inspiration.

Introduction to the
Paperback Edition

The cliché about the war between the sexes has, like all
clichés, its grain of truth: this war has its propaganda
and its blind patriotism. When the maps and alliances and
battle lines are drawn, loyalties pledged, sides declared, all
ambiguities, doubts, and subtleties seem to disappear. This
is a war of absolutes.

It often seems that when we stray into the world of
sexual politics every gesture is exaggerated, every conflict
magnified. Our conversations so easily turn into arguments, thoughts become polemics, pulses race, passions
rise. Everything takes place in an atmosphere of high
drama and courtroom spectacle; a penis is found next to a
highway and in every living room is a televised testimony
about date rape from a woman with a gray dot over her
face.

In September 1993 the small progressive college Antioch was catapulted to national attention by its extraordinary code of sexual conduct. As most people know, the

code requires spoken permission for every stage of a sexual encounter: intimate acts must be punctuated by questions like Can I kiss you? Can I unbutton your shirt? and so forth. The reason this code was applauded, condemned, discussed, and marveled at on television, on the front page of the *New York Times,* and in magazines and newspapers all over the world was not so much because it matters what a small group of students in Ohio do on a Friday night, but because the Antioch rules articulated the more diffuse attitudes about sexuality that had been floating around the culture at large. With their strange rules, the students and administrators at Antioch described something for us; they gave us a way to talk about how entwined sex and violence have become in our minds. They told us what we already know: we are a culture infatuated with the idea of consent.

A well-known feminist lectures all over America and Britain about "how to make consent sexy," but how sexy consent is or isn't or can be is not the point. The Antioch code of conduct represents a sort of Orwellian nightmare of cameras in the bedroom. The Antioch rules hold a mirror to our stranger preoccupations: they show us reflected in its crudest forms our desperate wish for rules about sex.

The irony is that along with the rise in rules comes a decline in responsibility. In the pages of this book, devoted to the idea of women taking responsibility for their actions, I am writing against the grain. Moral and legal responsibility are not in vogue for anybody these days — it is never our fault or our responsibility, it is always low self-esteem or social oppression or our family or patterns of abuse. If we cannot trust ourselves to be responsible, we have to rely on courts and on ever-more-elaborate codes of conduct. Once the individual is not held accountable for his or her behavior, it makes a certain amount of sense that we should look to new, stringent rules of sexual conduct to keep order.

In a twisted and paradoxical way, the preoccupation with sexual rules represents an almost utopian faith in our ability to create a safe sexual world. Like the Antioch rules, our intense concern with definitions of sexual harassment over the past few years demonstrates a deep-felt desire for — and belief in — a neat separation between sex and danger. In this time of sexual suspicion, changing roles, and disease, we seem to believe that somewhere out there is an instruction manual, a potent mixture of law and etiquette, that will tell us how to lead our sexual lives.

But the desire to regulate sex is not confined to what is appropriate to say to an office mate or what must be whispered at intimate moments. Even the imagination is expected to stoop before rules about sex and gender. In his latest thriller, *Disclosure*, Michael Crichton strays from the brittle and familiar images of male aggressors and female victims. He tells the story of a female boss who makes a pass at a male employee; he resists, she presses charges of sexual harassment, and everyone believes her because she is a woman. *Unrealistic* was the cry raised by many critics. They were right, of course; Crichton's plot does not unfold along the lines of the classic sexual harassment case. But what his critics seem to have forgotten is that *Disclosure* is a novel, a work of fiction. Michael Crichton has no obligation to what is euphemistically called realism and is actually something more like political acceptability. When he wrote *Jurassic Park,* no one complained that dinosaurs don't really roam the earth. But treading on the delicate ground of gender relations, Crichton does not have the same kind of literary freedom. A critic at the *Los Angeles Times* complained that she felt as if Crichton were cutting ahead of a line that women have been waiting in for a long time. What she was articulating with this strange image was her sense that Crichton was somehow breaking the rules. Anticipating this line of attack with commercial zeal, Crichton felt he had to include an afterword in his book responding to, and in fact almost apologizing for, his lack of "realism." He had to defend his subject matter against the accusation that he was somehow cutting in front of that long line for victim status.

It is dangerous to judge a book, any book, from supermarket thrillers to *Ulysses,* on how politically acceptable it is. As countless writers and theorists from Horace to Shelley have written, art is supposed to give us the familiar made new, not offer us what we already know warmed over. But what sparked the ire of Crichton's critics was precisely his desire to imagine something beyond the mundane black-and-white newsprint of ordinary experience. Like Crichton's dinosaurs, his characters crash through the stereotypes we seem to be so enthralled by: he was suggesting that sometimes women want sex and sometimes men don't, that men are not guilty simply because they are men and women are not beyond reproach simply because they are women.

Louis Menand expressed a similar sentiment in an eloquent essay in the *New Yorker:* "We have fallen into the belief that morality can be ascribed to groups. But groups cannot be moral or immoral: 'women' are not more or less moral than 'men,' and 'the city of Los Angeles' is not more or less moral than 'inner city youth.' Morality is an attribute only of persons." Although these seem to be simple and logical statements, we have reached the point in public discussion where the idea that one group is not more morally pure than another can no longer be taken for granted. In the current political atmosphere, commonsense statements like Menand's have been transformed into controversy and revelation.

How have we arrived at a place where banal assertions like "All men are not potential rapists" are worth hundreds of letters to an author? The answer seems to me to be that as a culture we have become astonishingly intolerant of dissent. I don't use words like "dissent" easily. To me the word seems like something dragged down from the attic, still dusty from the 1930s and harsh exchanges about Trotsky and Stalin in New York leftist circles. But having spent months strenuously trying to communicate my thoughts, I am convinced that we have to start thinking about dissent again. Of course, tolerating dissent does not mean agreeing with everything. It does not mean welcoming every idea with open arms like a hypocritical hostess. Tolerating dissent simply means that we sit with foreign ideas, the way we might with foreign people, long enough to hold a conversation, long enough for the differences between us to rise and expand, fully clarified and articulated. Tolerating dissent is allowing for the give-and-take, push and pull of intellectual conflict; it is the willing suspension of disbelief in order to allow ideas that are not our own to sharpen our perceptions.

I have sat through discussions with prominent feminists where tolerating dissent appears to mean nothing more than forcing agreement. As we talked about politics around a large round table, the majority would not permit differences of opinion to form and surface. When true differences threatened to puncture the surface of placid conversation, they would loudly declare agreement and lapse into the bland generalizations of consensus. In that setting, the toleration of dissent began to seem like something that would be produced by George Orwell's Ministry of Truth.

Most of us think of the free expression of ideas as desirable, at least in theory. For many Americans, dissent evokes a grand democratic tradition, the enthusiasm born at the wooden desks of fifth-grade classrooms where we memorized the Declaration of Independence and learned about the Boston Tea Party. Freedom of expression is a part of our abstract idea of what America is. The toleration of dissent is part of what we fight wars for and what the American flag means when we plant it on the moon. In practice, though, it doesn't come as naturally.

Today's intolerance of dissent is clever and protean. It takes different forms. Sometimes it is Gloria Steinem snapping "We don't give a shit about what she thinks" in a feminist forum when someone asked her about Camille Paglia; it is heckling a speaker as she is trying to deliver a speech; it is talking with absolute confidence about the content of a book without having read it.

But sometimes our intolerance is more subtle. It animates phrases like "You are not living in the real world." Banishing someone from the "real world" offers a way to dismiss him or her without having to respond to the substance of the argument. Of course one can divide the world infinitely into parts, suburbs versus city, office versus factory, universities versus McDonald's, but none of these worlds is more real than another. "Real" is one of those big bland vague words that seem powerful but are utterly lacking in descriptive value. Claiming that the inhabitants of the suburbs are less real than the inhabitants of the city or that university professors are less real than the manager of McDonald's is not a penetrating critical insight. When people declare their citizenship in the real world — which always involves denying someone else's — they are generally using the word "real" as a euphemism for "gritty." Drawing on the hollowest rhetoric of the 1960s, they are declaring that one can write with authority only if one has come from a background that is socially disadvantaged enough. The real-world argument has distant cousins like "Your grandmother was not a factory worker" or "You are writing from a position of privilege." The idea that such facts, in and of themselves, are enough to disqualify someone from writing has spread from academia into the larger culture.

Another form of intolerance that has its origins in academia is the insistence on a type of politicized language, on words like "patriarchy" or "gender, race, and class." Such language offers easy code words for "on our side." Automatically dismissing any book written in a different way is a form of evasion; it supplies the reader with another reason not to consider an argument, not to meet it on its own terms. What is ominous about this particular form of intolerance is that it dictates a certain homogeneity. The concept of the individual writer thinking ragged individual thoughts, writing in his or her own ragged individual idiom, is sacrificed to the idea of the sleek political mechanism churning out endless, methodical analyses written in the common language.

Intolerance of dissent also breathes life into words like "the backlash." Words like this force a confrontation. They offer a choice: embrace the article or book or book review in question as truth or dismiss it entirely. In an age of fast food and microwave ovens, it seems natural to reach for the equivalent in ideas. It is tempting — convenient, really — to glance at an article and immediately categorize it as ours or theirs without bothering to think it through.

But nothing interesting can come out of cultural discussions that are right against wrong, as appealing as they seem. They satisfy us, like watching sports or footage of wars. There is no doubt that it is somehow reassuring, and maybe more entertaining, to watch the forces of darkness battle the forces of light without any twinges of doubt about which is which. But tolerating dissent is about sustaining that doubt, keeping it alive long enough to come to one's own conclusions.

Intolerance of dissent disguises itself most convincingly in the argument that a book like this one might "fall into the wrong hands." Countless people have raised the concern that this book will be "used by the enemy." This anxiety is based on the assumption that the Rush Limbaughs and Ronald Reagans and Pat Buchanans of the world need a book like mine to justify their ways. They don't.

The lethal belief that we should not publicly think or analyze or question our assumptions is the contemporary version of what people said to Philip Roth. He shouldn't publish his novels about Jewish families, no matter how good they were, no matter how many glints of truth people saw in them, because they were "bad for the Jews." But what is bad for the Jews or for women or for the culture at large is if we have reached a point where we are not supposed to express our views.

If feminism is going to be a vital movement, then it is going to have to be able to sustain critique, not just critiques like "We should be able to wear lipstick" but critiques that are unsettling, critiques that shake us. By definition true dissent is disturbing, uncomfortable — it is precisely what we don't want to hear — but without it we can never get to a place where our exchange of insults becomes an exchange of ideas.

No matter how much we might like to, we can't control what the enemy reads. We can't control how the enemy interprets what it reads. The enemy has lots of information available to it, but then so do we. But the enemy doesn't really read for ambiguities, people tell me, the enemy reads for simple messages it can use for its own dark purposes. Perhaps this assumption about the enemy conceals an admission about ourselves: very few of us are reading for anything other than absolutes. It seems to me that we need to worry less about the enemy and more about ourselves and our ability to read and consume ideas that are not our own. The real enemy, as far as I am concerned, is that which inspires us to be quiet, cautious, and acceptable.

I don't think that there is anything particularly outrageous in the pages of this book, anything worthy of the fury it inspired. But it happened to fall into a cultural discussion that, aside from the lone dissenting voice of Camille Paglia, was not really a discussion at all. On issues like sexual harassment and date rape, there has been one accepted position in the mainstream media recycled and given back to us again and again in slightly different forms.

We have to see our way past the rules of the discussion. We have to invent ways to talk about politics and sex and responsibility that allow for independence of thought. We should owe allegiance only to what is vivid, original, and interesting. We should owe allegiance only to what feels true.

As the conversation opens up to more and varied voices, I hope there will be room for the jostling of ideas, for nuances and complexities, for speculations and ruminations, not just for the sound and the fury.

May 1994

The
Morning
After

Introduction

My grandmother lived in a world of manicures, hair salons, and no place to go in the morning. She shopped and played endless card games, the king and queen of hearts, spades, clubs, and diamonds absorbing all of her intellectual energy. She was caught in a bad marriage with nothing to fill her days. She missed feminism, my mother told me, by only a few years. It would have saved her.

So when I was very young I thought of feminism as something like a train you could catch and ride to someplace better. My grandmother missed it, but my mother caught it. I knew it was all about having your own work, before work meant anything to me but the sound of my mother's typewriter behind closed doors. In the sixties, my mother had written *Up the Sandbox*, an early feminist novel recounting the elaborate escape fantasies of a bored housewife. Feminism had a lot to do with my mother's own escapes, I knew that.

3

She would never let my younger sister and me watch *The Brady Bunch*, because it was sexist. Everyone else seemed to be watching the exotic row of blond girls file through their adventures, and we felt like we were missing something. When we finally managed to persuade her to let us watch an episode, she would hover over us reminding us that girls shouldn't want to be just cheerleaders.

My grandmother used to tell my mother that when you're on a date you should laugh at a boy's jokes, you should make conversation about the things he is interested in, and you should pretend everything he says is interesting even if it's not. You see, it was more complicated back then, my mother told me, now you just have to be interesting yourself.

My younger sister and I went to an all-girls school for thirteen years. As we neared high school we began to complain about being sequestered from the normal libidinous jostle of coeducation. We wanted boys in our classes. But our father said he wanted his daughters to learn to speak their mind. So we learned to speak our mind instead of worrying what the boy in the third row might think, much to our dismay.

This is where I come from. I didn't spend much time thinking about feminism. It was something assumed, something deep in my foundations. When I got to Harvard in the fall of 1986, all of that changed. I found something called feminism that was unfamiliar to me. The feminism around me in classrooms, conversations, and student journals was not the feminism I grew up with. The Take Back the Night marches and the sexual harassment peer-counseling groups were alien, and even sometimes at odds with what I thought feminism was. All of a sudden feminism meant being angry about men looking at you in the street and writing about "the colonialist appropriation of the female discourse."

At Harvard, and later at graduate school in English literature at Princeton, I was surprised at how many things there were not to say, at the arguments and assertions that could not be made, lines that could not be crossed, taboos that could not be broken. The feminists around me had created their own rigid orthodoxy. You couldn't question the existence of a rape crisis, you couldn't suggest that the fascination with sexual harassment had to do with more than sexual harassment, you couldn't say that Alice Walker was just a bad writer, and the list of couldn'ts went on and on. Listening to feminist conversations, in and out of class, I was surprised at how fenced in they were, how little territory there was that could actually be disputed.

I remember sitting through a workshop on date rape freshman year, thinking, This is not me, this has nothing to do with me. The naive female victim in the film being shown was worlds away. Her fifties-style dates were not the kind of dates my older sisters went on. She was passive and innocent, and overly impressed by the boy's intelligence. She didn't drink. It might as well have been a documentary about the mating habits of the fruit fly. The thing I didn't know then was that the mating rituals of a rape-sensitive community, and the attitudes that went along with them, would be a part of feminism as I would experience it from then on.

A new bedroom politics had entered the university. Fighting date rape and sexual harassment seemed to unite and inspire the feminists around me. Everything was cut-and-dried. It was feminists against the backlash, us against them, and increasingly I was "them."

As I see it, there are more than two sides to any issue, and feminists are closer to their backlash than they'd like to think. The image that emerges from feminist preoccupations with rape and sexual harassment is that of women as victims, offended by a professor's dirty joke, verbally pressured into sex by peers. This image of a delicate woman bears a striking resemblance to that fifties ideal my mother and the other women of her generation fought so hard to get away from. They didn't like her passivity, her wide-eyed innocence. They didn't like the fact that she was perpetually offended by sexual innuendo. They didn't like her excessive need for protection. She represented personal, social, and psychological possibilities collapsed, and they worked and marched, shouted and wrote, to make her irrelevant for their daughters. But here she is again, with her pure intentions and her wide eyes. Only this time it is the feminists themselves who are breathing new life into her.

This book is not a scientific survey of campus life, measuring the immeasurable with statistical certainty. This is not a comprehensive, encyclopedic sociological analysis.

It is not a political polemic. I am not a camera, to invert Christopher Isherwood's famous narrative metaphor; I cannot offer the objective truth, unfiltered through my own opinion. I have written what I see, limited, personal, but entirely real. I have written my impressions.

This book comes out of frustration, out of anger, out of the names I've been called, out of all the times I didn't say something I was thinking because it might offend the current feminist sensibility. But there is something else — my grandmother and her card games, her hands turning over card after card, dealing faster and faster, memorizing numbers. It is out of the deep belief that some feminisms are better than others that I have written this book.

The Blue-Light System

With its magnolia trees, its gray Gothic buildings, Princeton's pastoral campus looks like it hasn't changed much over the last century. But when the sun goes down, it's clear that the last five years have altered the face of the campus. There are still freshmen wandering around late at night, but there are also blue lights up all over campus in case someone pulls you into the darkness. The blue lights above security phones — part of what is often called the blue-light system — were erected on many campuses in the eighties. Since the phones aren't actually used much for emergencies, their primary function seems to be to reassure the lone wanderer. Having started with fifteen lights and added some each year, Princeton now has around seventy. The blue lights mark a new and systematic sense of danger. People may have always been scared walking around campuses late at night, but now, bathed in blue light, they are officially scared.

As freshmen in the late eighties and early nineties, we

arrive at college amid a flurry of warnings: "Since you cannot tell who has the potential for rape by simply looking, be on your guard with every man." "Do not put yourself in vulnerable situations." "Condoms are not perfect and they do not provide '*safe sex*.' " "To eliminate risk, abstain from sex or avoid sexual intimacy beyond fantasy, massage and mutual masturbation." "Over fifty percent of all female college students experience some form of sexual victimization or sexual harassment." "No birth control is one hundred percent effective except the word 'NO!' " "Are you hearing LOVE when your boyfriend is saying SEX?" "One in four college women has experienced rape or attempted rape since age fourteen."[1]

As we are settling into our new surroundings, there are fliers and counselors and videotapes telling us how not to get AIDS and how not to get raped, where not to wander and what signals not to send. By the end of freshman week, we know exactly what not to do. Once we make it through the workshops and pamphlets on date rape, safe sex, and sexual harassment, no matter how bold and adolescent, how rebellious and reckless, we are left with an impression of imminent danger. And then there are the whistles. Female freshmen arriving at Wesleyan and other campuses are given whistles to protect them against rape and assault. For the past couple of years at Princeton, there has been someone outside the building during registration offering these whistles to female students on their way out.

Several years ago, parents and prospective students on tours of the Wesleyan campus saw more of college life than they expected. As they were touring the campus, looking at the library and the classrooms, the students playing Frisbee on the grass and the freshman dorms, the cheerful patter of the tour guide was interrupted by the impassioned words of a feminist student. She delivered a three-minute speech about the danger of rape, warning parents and prospective students to take the university's response to the rape crisis into consideration when applying to college. She urged them to ask the administration questions about security and blue lights. The rape crisis is not just at Wesleyan but everywhere, she told them.

That spring she and another student involved in this dramatic effort at what would have once been called consciousness-raising disrupted many tours, raising the ire of the administration. Parents and prospective students were shaken. Needless to say, the admissions office was not happy to have the issue of date rape thrust at students on the brink of their decision about colleges. Parents, already worried about sending their children to a strange place, had another source of concern to add to their list. But the guerrilla feminists were effective in their purpose: they successfully planted the fear of rape in the minds of prospective students before they even reached the Wesleyan campus.

Word of mouth, then, comes from older students as well as university staff. The barrage of warnings is not just the product of a bureaucratic mechanism churning out pieces of paper. The warnings are not just official university policy filtering down to us from above. There are faces and stories behind these warnings. They have taken hold of student attention. Students run women's centers and hot lines, workshops and peer-counseling groups. They write plays and design videos and posters about rape. Campus literary magazines and political journals are filled with stories and poems about sexual danger. Most visibly, most dramatically, students organize and march against rape.

I remember myself, a bewildered freshman, watching candle-lit faces weave snakelike through campus. Angry voices were chanting "Two, four, six, eight, no more date rape," and the marchers carried signs saying "Take Back the Night." I remember an older student from my high school, whom I'd always respected, always thought particularly glamorous, marching, her face flushed with emotion, and I wondered what it was about. Before the chants condensed into meaning, when they were still sounds instead of words, I wondered whom they wanted the night back from and what they wanted it back for. The confusion was not just mine. The vague poetic symbols of the campus movement against rape speak of a more general fear. As the marchers passed, I wandered back to my dorm through the still-unfamiliar campus, the darkness suddenly charged with a nameless threat.

◈

In this era of Just Say No and No Means No, we don't have many words for embracing experience. Now instead of liberation and libido, the emphasis is on trauma and disease. Now the idea of random encounters, of joyful, loveless sex, raises eyebrows. The possibility of adventure is clouded by the specter of illness. It's a difficult backdrop for conducting one's youth.

What further complicates sexual existence is that the sexual revolution hasn't been entirely erased by a new ethos of sexual conservatism. Free love hasn't been entirely eclipsed by safe sex. Sexual climates do not move across our experience like cold fronts on a weather map. Instead, they linger and accumulate. Today's culture of caution co-exists with yesterday's devil-may-care. Encouraged, discouraged, condemned, condoned, youthful sexual activity is met with powerful and conflicting responses. Everywhere we look there are signs of sexual puritanism, but there are also signs of sexual abandon. Adding to the mixed messages are signs of sexual danger.

On the subway, next to a condom ad in Spanish, there is an ad for perfume showing a naked man carrying a naked woman over his shoulder. On an average day we are flooded with images of erotic promise: the topless couple in a Calvin Klein underwear ad; a poster of an ecstatic Madonna with her stomach bare, her jeans unbuttoned, her book, *Sex*, on the cover of *Newsweek*; the pornographic section of our video store; the XXX movie houses in certain neighborhoods; men with long hair, chests bare, arms around each other, in an advertisement for Banana Republic — and the list goes on. We may not always notice these images, but like buildings and trees, they are part of our landscape.

This is a culture that pulls both ways. Pat Buchanan rails about the importance of sexual morality, and Banana Republic uses sex to sell clothes. We've been hearing Reagan and then Bush drone on about family values for as long as we can remember, but we haven't lost the myth of the casual encounter. Pressures clash. Our ears were filled simultaneously with Nancy Reagan's Just Say No and George Michael's late-eighties hit song "I Want Your Sex." An image from deep childhood perfectly captures today's conflicted sexual climate: Dr. Dolittle's two-headed creature, the *pushmi-pullyu*.

There's no doubt that some people are running around thinking only about pleasure and whom they're going to go home with after a party. But that is not the whole story. Many are more concerned with getting ahead and getting a nice car than getting drunk and getting laid. The pressure to do well and make money in an age of diminishing economic expectations looms larger than it did for those who went to college in the sixties and seventies.

Finding yourself pales in comparison to supporting your-self. These days desire is often tailored by a preprofessional pragmatism, and many undergraduates, although not nec-essarily the ones I knew, are keeping their lives, sexually and otherwise, in relative order.

Yes, they are arguing about whether to teach absti-nence in New York City's public schools, and yes, there are more pressures to stay faithful and stay at home, but we still haven't lost the idea of the sexual revolution. We still hear stories from older brothers, sisters, cousins, and aunts about sleeping around and not caring, and feeling free and pretending to feel free.

I remember, when I was young, hearing my older sister tell my mother that she was the last person on earth who was faithful to her husband. I turned to look at my mother, imagining her as a dinosaur, the kind they keep at the Mu-seum of Natural History. Everyone else, my sister told me, was into free love and all that. I remember exactly where we were sitting when we had that conversation. I remem-ber the color of the couch. And I remember the visions of having dozens of husbands, like a bouquet of flowers, run-ning through my mind.

The sexual revolutionaries, then, have made their im-pression, and we are still impressed. Warnings about sex-ual harassment and sexual disease compete with wanton images of sexual freedom. Even though attitudes toward sexual experimentation have changed, many people still think of it as a necessary stage. We are still intrigued and pressured and exhausted by the sexual revolution. Although we may have developed an almost blasé attitude toward the absolute ideals of libertinism, they still exert a strong presence in the way we think and the choices we make.

People tell me that sex should be as free as it was not so long ago, that we shouldn't have to use discretion and condoms. We may have been thinking about AIDS for about as long as we've been thinking about sex, but many of us still expect to experiment. While there is a strong cultural belief that sexual adventure is a minefield of rape and disease, there is also a lingering refrain: this is not the way it's supposed to be.

The shift from free love to safe sex is itself part of our experience. Our sexual climate, then, incorporates the movement from one set of sexual mores to another. The presence of the past complicates our decisions. Messages mix, and our imaginations catch hold of one, then the other, dragging our bodies this way and that.

I remember the parties, dark rooms, beer, cigarettes, dancing shadows dressed in mostly black. In the corner a vodka punch, with a cherry taste. Girls were dancing with girls, some because they were interested in each other, others because they were trying to catch the attention of the boy across the room. That spring, girls had started taking their shirts off at parties. I remember the bras, black lace, white lace, pink lace. There was a drama in dancing in bras, in crushing taboos beneath our feet. For most people, boys were in the background those nights. They were not the point. Dancing without shirts was intended as a bold statement about the triumph of the female body, an eye-catching, spirit-lifting display of sexual availability. As music surged, as bodies pressed against each other, it was a show of sexuality, freedom, and power, a charade of earlier, wilder days. We definitely had something to prove, and beneath all the bacchanalian urgency, there was something calculating, something self-conscious, something designed to impress. But what was there to prove in the dark room surrounded by people who had eaten breakfast, lunch, and dinner together every day for years? The point, I think, was to exhibit a power, as well as a freedom we didn't quite have. In the dark, without shirts, it was ourselves we were trying to impress. It was, above all, a dance of control, and the rhythm was frustration.

That same spring, most of the shirtless dancers would shout about date rape until they were hoarse at Take Back the Night. To many observers the conjunction of these two activities seemed contradictory, even hypocritical. But dancing without shirts and marching at Take Back the Night are, strange as it seems, part of the same parade. The different drums of sexual desirability, strength and vulnerability, frustration and fear, are all part of the group exhibitionism: the same show of power, and the same dance of control.

◈

Liquor and parties still hold their allure for the freshman, but it's an allure full of complications and second thoughts. Hormones run high at this age, but they mix uneasily with worry. Maybe the freshman hasn't had much experience with boys. Maybe her parents were strict about curfews. In jeans, lipstick, and a tight black shirt, maybe she's finally at a real party with upperclassmen.

This is a generic story. Our freshman gets a beer, and a handsome boy from one of her classes, she doesn't remember which, comes up and flirts with her. She smiles at him, and in that instant she tries to calculate the risks. She tries to remember which girl she saw him with last week. She looks at his torn jeans — he looks bisexual, he looks like he might be one of those sullen-youth types who have spent a summer in the East Village injecting heroin. People are dancing to the pounding music, "However do you want me. However do you need me." The music makes it hard to hear each other, and he suggests they go up to his room to talk.

She hesitates. Flashes of the play she just saw about date rape run through her head. His invitation evokes the black-and-white print of the manual warning her about

AIDS. Someone she knows has just caught herpes. All around her people are dancing. Her drink is beginning to blur the edges of her vision. Maybe she goes with him, maybe she doesn't, but either way the situation is complicated. Pleasure is charged with danger, safety with regret.

For both male and female college students, the usual drive toward sexual experience collides with the powerful drive against it. No matter how you choose to behave when it comes down to it at midnight on a Saturday, the conflicting pressures and contemporary taboos are with you in one way or another.

These pressures and taboos leave their traces all over campuses, in conversations and classrooms, in meetings and on bathroom walls. In the women's bathroom in the basement of the Princeton library, someone has scribbled "Sex is death," and in another bathroom someone has written "Sex is rape." These extreme and dramatic aphorisms spring from a fierce suspicion of sex. For most seventeen-year-olds college opens up a whole realm of sexual possibility, and some of the attention lavished on the darker, violent side of sex comes from a deep ambivalence about what that freedom actually entails.

In another Princeton bathroom, someone has written "There is no such thing as safe sex," and underneath it someone has added in bold letters, "Isolation is the best protection." Another person asks the communal wall, "Are you scared walking around late at night?" Several scribblers have answered yes.

At Wesleyan, the bathroom walls are filled with written conversations about rape and sexual harassment. Some people have named names, and there are comments back and forth. At Carleton College, in the bathroom on the third floor of the library, there is a list of alleged date rapists, popularly referred to as the "castration list."[2] Brown has a similar list. These lists are intended to allow victims to voice their experience in a safe, anonymous space. They enable victims to accuse without confrontation and consequences. Several campuses have erected "Walls of Shame" with a similar, though more public purpose, and at Columbia, students have posted the names of alleged date rapists on pieces of paper all over campus.

From cynical truisms about sex to written exchanges about date rape, on these campus walls expressions of sexuality are mingled with fear. The message is about danger and safety, about the perceived conflict between sex and well-being. Students have lost their faith in the simplicity of the sexual encounter, in the do-what-you-want-and-don't-worry-about-it mentality. The proverbial locker room is cluttered with a whole new set of sexual anxieties. These graffiti writers aren't worried about enough "freedom" anymore — they are worried about too much danger.

At Princeton, on an average morning, the gym is more crowded than the library. Many of the girls lifting weights and riding the Exercycle are not just trying to be healthy and strong; many of them are obsessed with the shape of their body. The pressures and costs of being conventionally attractive revolve with every whirl of the Exercycle, with every futile step of the Stairmaster. As wheels are spinning and sun is hitting the scale in the gym, these girls, hearts beating faster, sweat running, stomachs getting flatter, legs thinner, are pursuing an impossible ideal. Some of them can't stop running, or Exercycling, or Stairmastering. These are the ones who develop serious eating disorders.

You see them walk around campus, pale, with circles under their eyes, their limbs fragile as twigs. There are so many of them, more than ever before. These girls are afflicted with anorexia, a paradoxical obsession with societal standards of glamour as thinness combined with an effective evasion of sexuality. After they have starved themselves, they don't look like women anymore. They latch on to social pressure to be thin, and therefore sexy, and distort that pressure beyond recognition. They get thin beyond any definition of sexy. These girls effectively put themselves out of the sexual game.

Anorexia, then, represents, among other things, the burning desire to be attractive, combined with the burning desire to not be attractive. As Naomi Wolf correctly, if melodramatically, points out in *The Beauty Myth*, there is a surprisingly large population of anorexics fleeing from adult sexuality as it manifests itself in our culture. With their emaciated androgyny, they are turning back the clock. They have created a way to not be women, to not face the bewildering onslaught of sexual activity.

Of course there are psychological reasons that each individual is bent on starvation and self-destruction, but the growing prevalence of anorexia also says something about the cultural outlets available for personal craziness. The presence of so many anorexics in our universities provides painful physical evidence of the kind of sexual paralysis that arises from the urgent and contradictory messages about sex: sex is the most important thing in the world, sex is a fashion model in the pages of *Vogue*, sex brings danger, sex is, in one in four cases, against your will.

The extremes of anorexia are relatively rare, but the obsession with weight and body in its milder forms is not. Although most people don't go as far as anorexia, lots of women have at one time or another devoted so much energy to their body and diet that they haven't had much energy left over for work or friends, let alone men. They turn their attention, concentrated, obsessive, inward on their own body, effectively eluding the pressures of the outside world.

In a safe-sex workshop, college students sit in a circle and participate in role-playing games. The roles are handed out on slips of paper. Two students get up and act out the scene: you have to convince the boy you've been going out with for a month that you won't have sex with him unless he uses a condom. You have to convince the girl you've just started a relationship with that you want to use condoms even though she's on the pill. When the cautious role player convinces the reckless role player, everyone else applauds.

The safe-sex group leaders talk about ways to make safe sex less embarrassing. They talk about ways to make the other person feel comfortable about discussing condoms. They even talk about how to make condom use erotic. The focus is on condom skills. At some places they even go so far as to practice putting a condom on a banana with their eyes covered, to prove they can do it in the dark.

When discussing safe sex, which they've accepted in theory if not in practice, students in the workshop talk about trust. One offers the solution of telling the man that you trust him, but you just don't trust the other women he's slept with. After all, as the grim and somewhat perverse warning goes, if you have sex with someone, you have sex with all of their past sexual partners too. People talk about being clean, as in "Most people at Princeton are clean." As the students talk about whom they trust and who's clean, their language slips into the language of judgment. They talk about the right (safe) thing and the wrong (risky) thing in absolute, moral terms. The group moves through the topics in total unity. There is no room for individual opinion.

As the students sit in the circle, wearing nametags, no

one says he or she doesn't use condoms. No one says that when it's dark and you've had a few drinks, you don't care. Someone bravely says he knows people who don't use condoms. No one mentions that it's hard to interrupt the fiction of romance, the fleeting escape of the casual encounter, to say: I think you may have a disease. I look for signs of frustration, rebellion, dissent, but there are only heads nodding in consensus. Any conflict these students may have about the new sexual ethos remains largely unspoken, buried beneath the chorus of "If you respect your partner . . . If you respect yourself . . ." One freshman says that she won't have sex unless her partner gets tested first. Although some of the girls are worried about being forward, everyone agrees that it's important to carry condoms. Within this closed circle, in the basement of University Health Services, under fluorescent lights, sex without condoms is an unspeakable sin.

"Did you use a condom?" we would ask each other over breakfast. "You really should have used a condom with *him*." In Adams House, my college dorm, we had a Christmas tree in the dining hall decorated with condoms. Its branches were laden with different kinds — ribbed, fiesta-colored, mint-flavored. People talked a lot about condoms, especially freshman and sophomore year. People grumbled about them, "It's like taking a shower with a raincoat." Student organizations passed them around. People gave them away as party favors. We carried them around in bags, and pockets and wallets. Some of us even used them, sometimes. But mainly condoms were protective amulets. We laughed about them, played with them, even celebrated them as part of our bravado, but they were emblems of danger, tiny representations of a larger, abstract fear.

Most straight college students don't actually think they're going to get AIDS. Most of us probably think of it as a disease out there for somebody else. Lots of people I know don't think much about all the condoms they could have used or that night last year when they got swept up in the moment and weren't as careful as they might have been. I remember a friend telling me that our chances of actually getting AIDS were about the same as the chance a piano would fall on our head. He said he read that somewhere.

AIDS may not brush directly against our lives, it may not get us to use condoms or avoid mysterious strangers, but it does suggest, somewhere in the recesses of ego, if not id, the possibility of sexually transmitted death. If AIDS doesn't affect our actions — and it doesn't always — then it affects the way we think about our actions.

Rational or irrational, some of the people I know outside of risk groups worry about having AIDS. An itch, a bump, a boil, a stubborn cold, a sore ankle, and people worry. They think about that person they really shouldn't have slept with — complicated regrets crowding into a narrow fear — and they become obsessed with the possibility that they might have gotten AIDS. However tangible or diffuse, the sense of danger hovers over our experience,

24

inevitably affecting our bedrooms, and our politics, and our mornings after.

Unlike the sexual dangers of the past, syphilis and illegal abortion among them, this peril is not borne in whispers and rumors, it is not unspoken, it is not taboo. The AIDS epidemic is now paraded before us, in newspapers, magazines, and advertisements and at dinner parties. Millions of teenagers have watched the threat of AIDS penetrate even the sheltered, clean-cut television world of *Beverly Hills, 90210.* Which goes to show that even the most shallow, sanitized, whitewashed of contexts is not immune to mentions of the virus.

Each day in the paper there is new information about side effects of a new treatment and some new protest about AIDS research. Some mornings I skip those articles. I go on to read the weather report or the movie reviews, but the images of AIDS are hard to repress or avoid. It's hard to close the newspaper, turn off the television, pass the man on the street with a sign saying he has AIDS, without noticing. The article, the picture, the man with the sign, stay with me, the people I know who have gotten it stay with me. Even if I think to myself I'll never get it, over and over, words of reassurance, even if I think I am not at risk, I'll never catch it, I can do whatever I want, nothing can catch me, it is still there.

Whether or not we actually alter our behavior, we still see the direct link between sex and death mapped out again and again, in molecular diagrams, obituaries, and photographs of the sick. Our parents send us articles clipped out of the paper: "NICE GIRL FROM RESPECTABLE NEW YORK CITY PREP SCHOOL GETS AIDS."

As a senior, I watched the street outside of Adams House fill with Take Back the Night marchers, feeling the swell of emotion. Many people I knew were out marching. They sat at recruiting tables in the dining hall for hours selling buttons. I wondered what it was in the chants, the signs, the candles — anger, frustration, fear — that was drawing such crowds. In the midst of social and sexual ambiguity, this is a movement that offers a rare clarity, that offers a no that means only no.

New incarnations of campus feminism shape and are shaped by the sexual climate. The fear of rape and the fear of AIDS contribute to the sense of danger. They both contribute to a rhetoric of caution, to how the freshman feels about the prospect of sexual relationships. There are reasons beyond the straightforward that pull thousands of women across the country to Take Back the Night marches each year. There is a purpose being served, a reason that the issue of date rape captures the energy, outrage, and fear of so many so passionately.

As Joan Didion wrote years ago about the women's movement, "The movement is no longer a cause but a symptom." The movement against date rape is a symptom of a more general anxiety about sex. The momentum it has gained in the past five years is in part a response to the added fear of AIDS. Take Back the Night offers tangible targets, things to chant against and rally around in a sexually ambiguous time. Take Back the Night is a symptom of conservative attitudes about sex mingling with the remains of the sexual revolution. The crisis is not a rape crisis, but a crisis in sexual identity.

When my mother was younger she memorized these lines of Edna St. Vincent Millay's: "My candle burns at both ends; / It will not last the night; / But, ah, my foes, and, oh, my friends — / It gives a lovely light." But now, faced with the medical reality of the shortened night, she doesn't think her daughters should burn the candle at both ends anymore. My own mother tells me that she really doesn't think anyone should have sex anymore unless they're in a long-term, monogamous relationship. Edna St. Vincent Millay's light, that hard, bright, hedonistic light, has lost some of its loveliness.

Someone tells me that at Wesleyan the blue lights were a source of struggle. Feminists fought hard over where and how many. They wanted more. One problem was the observatory in the middle of campus. The astronomers didn't want blue lights put up around it because the reflection interfered with their ability to see the stars. Feminists argued that their safety was more important than scientific dabbling. They argued that they couldn't walk through campus at night without blue lights around the observatory. Finally the feminists and the astronomers reached a compromise. Now there are blue lights around the obser-vatory, but they are a special kind, built low to the ground, so they won't disrupt astronomic observation.

A friend shows his younger sister around Princeton. She is perched on the precarious border between childhood and adolescence. She is bored by all the gray buildings, the modern statues and flowers; it is the blue lights that catch her attention. She has a headband just that color. She asks if the lights are for catching bugs. After some hesitation, some vagueness, her brother tells her what they're really for. In case someone attacks you. In case someone tries to rape you. In case. In the long process of learning what those lights are really for, she'll learn vulnerability and lurking dangers in the bushes. She'll learn to be afraid walking around at night. Maybe she'll even learn, as the pamphlet says, to "be on your guard with every man." There is something out there trying to get you. She'll learn all that.

Looking down from Fine Tower, the highest point at Princeton, the campus is dramatically dotted with glowing blue lights. They are eerie, beautiful, like fireflies. They signal reassurance and warning at the same time. Red means stop, green means go, and blue means be afraid.

Taking Back
the Night

It's April — leaves sprouting, flowers, mad crushes, flirtations, Chaucer's pilgrims, bare legs, long days, and marches against rape. Renewal means more than those practically obscene magnolia trees again, branches laden with Georgia O'Keeffe blossoms. Renewal means more than passing exams and drinking wine outside. It means more than enjoying the lengthening day: it means taking back the night.

It's a Saturday night. It's the end of the month and it still hasn't gotten warm. Instead of listening to bands, or watching movies, or drinking beer, more than four hundred Princeton students are "taking back the night." That is, they are marching, as one of the organizers says into the microphone, "to end sexual violence against women." In past years the numbers have climbed to a thousand participants. Carrying candles, the students march through campus, past the library, and down Prospect Street, past the eating clubs, the social hub of Princeton's undergraduates.

The marchers chant "Princeton unite, take back the night, Princeton unite, take back the night," and a drumbeat adds drama, noise, and substance to their voices. As they pass the eating clubs the chants get louder, more forceful. "No matter what we wear, no matter where we go, yes means yes and no means no!" It's already dark. They scheduled the march earlier this year, because last year's march went until three in the morning. "Hey ho! Hey ho! Sexism has got to go." As they march, girls put their arms around each other. Some of the march organizers wear armbands. This is to identify them in case anyone falls apart and needs to talk.

The ritual is this: at various points in the march everyone stops and gathers around the microphone. Then the "survivors" and occasionally the friends of "survivors" get up to "speak out." One by one they take their place at the microphone, and one by one they tell their story. The stories are intimate accounts of sexual violence, ranging from being afraid on the subway to having been the victim of gang rape and incest.

The marchers stand in Prospect Garden, a flower garden behind the faculty club. A short, plump girl who looks like she is barely out of high school cups her hands around the microphone. Her face is pink from the cold. She begins to describe a party at one of the eating clubs. Her words are slow, loud, deliberate. That night, she had more beers than she could remember, and she was too drunk to know what was going on. A boy she knew was flirting with her, he asked her to go back to his room — it all happened so fast. Her friends told her not to. They told her she was too drunk to make decisions. She went anyway, and he raped her. Later, she says, his roommates thought he was cool for "hooking up." She left her favorite blue jean jacket in his room. She finally went and got it back, but she never wore it again. She pauses. Later the boy apologized to her, so, she says angrily, he must have known it was rape. She stops talking and looks into the crowd. Everyone applauds to show their support.

As the applause dies down, another girl stands up, her face shiny with tears, and brushes the blond hair out of her eyes. I wasn't going to speak out, she explains, because I wasn't a survivor of rape, but I too was silenced. A friend, she continues, someone I used to have a crush on, betrayed my trust. We were lying next to each other and he touched my body. She pauses, swallowing the tears rising in her throat, then goes on: I didn't say anything, I was too embarrassed to say or do anything. I just pretended I was asleep. Distraught, confused, she talks in circles for a while, not sure where her story is leading her, and finally walks away from the microphone.

The next girl to speak out wears a leather jacket and black jeans. People think of me as a bitch, she says, her voice loud, confident, angry, they think of me as a slut. They think I treat men badly. But she explains that underneath her bitchiness is a gang rape that happened when she was sixteen. So if you see someone who acts like me, you shouldn't judge them or hate them, she says. Considering what happened to me I am in good shape, she says, I'm doing really well. It's just fucking great that I can even have orgasms. As she leaves the microphone, her friends put their arms around her.

People stand beneath Blair Arch, the final spot for the speak-outs. The night has gotten cold, but no one seems to notice. Even though baby-sitting has been arranged by the organizers, someone has brought a young child in a stroller. Above the marchers' heads is an open dorm window. Through it, we can hear the sounds of boys watching sports on television. Intermittently the survivors' stories are punctuated by the cheers of these boys — "Yeah!" and "All right!" — when something happens in their game. Their shouts, full of footballs and touchdowns, full of self-consciously virile joy in male strength, provide a strange background for stories about rape. To the marchers below, these shouts are unwitting demonstrations of masculinity at fault. As one boy says into the microphone, "This isn't (and shouldn't be) a good night to be a man."

Actually, nearly half of those present at the march are male. That has been true at Princeton almost every year. Although some may come out of curiosity, most seem to come to show solidarity. A few of the boys get up to say that they are also affected by sexual violence and proceed to tell stories about their girlfriend's being raped. A few talk about their own experiences of being molested as children by older men, but most tell vicarious stories. One boy with long hair and a long trench coat explains his particularly difficult case: he actually looked like a man who had raped his girlfriend, and the first time he kissed her she threw up.

One boy tells his own story about being afraid of sexual violence. He was seven, wandering around a mall, and he noticed that a man was following him, up and down the escalators, in and out of stores. He finally managed to get away, and through this experience, he says, he truly understands the experience of being a woman and being afraid.

A girl tells of being raped by a Frenchman when she was traveling in Europe. Several girls describe sexual violence in distant lands and foreign languages. A few tell of being molested by a relative. Someone tells of being raped in another country *and* being molested by a relative.

The strange thing is that as these different girls — tall and short, fat and thin, nervous and confident — get up to give intensely personal accounts, all of their stories begin to sound the same. Listening to a string of them, I hear patterns begin to emerge. The same phrases float through different voices. Almost all of them begin "I wasn't planning to speak out tonight but . . . ," even the ones who had spoken in previous years. They talk about feeling helpless, and feeling guilty. Some talk about hating their bodies. The echoes continue: "I didn't admit it or talk about it." "I was silenced." "I was powerless over my own body."

The catchwords travel across campuses, and across the boundaries between the spoken and written word. In a piece in the most radical of Harvard's feminist magazines, the *Rag*, one student asks, "Why should I have to pay with silence for a crime committed against my body? . . . I want you to know how it feels to be denied your own voice."[1] Voicelessness is a common motif in Take Back the Night speak-outs. In 1988 the *Daily Princetonian* quoted one speaker as saying, "Victims shouldn't be silenced."[2] At Berkeley, students organized a group designed to combat sexual assault called Coalition to Break the Silence.[3] In the *Nassau Weekly*, Jennifer Goode, a Princeton sophomore, writes that Take Back the Night "counteracts the enforced silence of everyday existence. . . . This Saturday night the silence will be broken."[4]

These Princeton women, future lawyers, newspaper reporters, investment bankers, are hardly the voiceless, by most people's definition. But silence is poetic. Being silenced is even more poetic. These days people vie for the position of being silenced, but being silenced is necessarily a construction of the articulate. Once you're talking about being voiceless, you're already talking. The first Take Back the Night march at Princeton was more than ten years ago, and every year they're breaking the silence all over again. The fashionable cloak of silence is more about style than content.

Built into the rhetoric about silence is the image of a malign force clamping its hands over the mouths of victims. This shadowy force takes on many names —

patriarchy, men, society — but with such abstract quantities in the formula, it's hard to fathom the meaning behind the metaphor. It doesn't matter, though. Almost all of the victims continue to talk about their silence.

It is the presumption of silence that gives these women the right to speak, that elevates their words above the competitive noise of the university. Silence is the passkey to the empowering universe of the disempowered. Having been silenced on today's campus is the ultimate source of authority.

One of the most scathing condemnations of the long-standing feminist obsession with silence comes from John Irving. In *The World According to Garp*, Irving tells the story of Ellen James, a modern-day Philomela: she was raped at the age of eleven, and her tongue was cut out by the rapist. Much to Garp's dismay, a group of feminists springs up around her, cutting out their own tongue in a gesture of political solidarity. They communicate through notes: "I am an Ellen Jamesian." They hold meetings and take stands. They dedicate themselves to the cause. When Ellen James herself reappears in the novel as an adult, she confesses that she hates the Ellen Jamesians. Beneath his comic, excessive, grotesque image of this feminist clan, Irving makes a realistic point about the feminist preoccupation with silence. He takes the political reality of feminists' insistence on identification with victims one step further: his feminists are so eager to declare themselves silenced that they are actually willing to cut out their own tongue.

As I listen to the refrains, "I have been silent," "I was silenced," "I am finally breaking the silence," the speakers begin to blur together in my mind. It makes sense that rape victims experience some similar reactions, but what is strange is that they choose the same words. Somehow the individual power of each story is sapped by the collective mode of expression. The individual details fade, the stories blend together, sounding programmed and automatic. As I listen to them I am reminded of the scene in Madeleine L'Engle's children's book *A Wrinkle in Time* in which a row of identical children play outside of a row of identical houses, bouncing a row of identical balls.

The *Rag*'s account of a rape ends "Thanks [to] the rest of you for listening," and an account published in the *Daily Princetonian* ends "Thank you for listening."[5] As the vocabulary shared across campuses reveals, there is an archetype, a model, for the victim's tale. Take Back the Night speak-outs follow conventions as strict as any sonnet sequence or villanelle. As intimate details are squeezed into formulaic standards, they seem to be wrought with an emotion more generic than heartfelt.

One theme that runs through all the speak-outs is self-congratulation — I have survived and now I am to be congratulated. Rhapsodies of self-affirmation may be part of "the healing practice," but as speaker after speaker praises herself for inner strength, they begin to seem excessive. From this spot in American culture, beneath Blair Arch at a Take Back the Night march, the population seems more oversaturated with self-esteem than with cholesterol. One common formulation at Take Back the Night is: "I am a survivor and it's a miracle every time I get a good grade, it's a miracle when I have friends, it's a miracle when I have relationships. It's a miracle. And I thank God every day." In the account in the *Daily Princetonian*, the survivor closes by saying, "If you don't know how to react next time you see me, give me a hug and tell me that you think I'm very brave. Because I, like all the other victims who speak out at Take Back the Night, am very brave."[6]

In the context of Take Back the Night, it is entirely acceptable to praise yourself for bravery, to praise yourself for recovery, and to praise yourself for getting out of bed every morning and eating breakfast. Each story chronicles yet another ascent toward self-esteem, yet another "revolution from within."

As survivors tell their stories, as people hold hands, as they march and chant, there is undoubtedly a cathartic release. There is a current of support between listeners and speakers. At Columbia last year, students waited on line for hours to tell their stories, and as they did the listeners would chant, "It's not your fault," "We believe you," "We love you," and "Tell your story." The energy runs through the applause and the tears, the candlelight and the drumbeats. This is the same energy that sells millions of self-help books every year. This is march as therapy.

In the words of Susan Teres, director of SHARE, Princeton's sexual harassment and assault-education and counseling program, the march is about "finding your own healing practices" and "taking back who you are and what you need and want. This is your journey, your reclaiming of a strong sense of self." The language is New Age mixed with recovery group. At the end of the march there is a moment of silence. Everyone holds hands. Afterward there is a midnight workshop, called Claiming the Vision: A Ritual of Healing and Commitment.

Some feminists argue that Take Back the Night thrusts the issue of safety, more blue lights, and more full-time rape counselors into the public eye. But the march also has its less practical dimension: its ritualistic, symbolic meaning that eclipses the nuts and bolts of specific demands. With its candles, its silence, its promise of transformations, this movement offers a substitute for religion. The symbol of Take Back the Night, emblazoned on T-shirts, buttons, and posters, is three women holding up the moon. All of that moon imagery seems strange, evoking latter-day earth goddesses roaming through Princeton's campus.

Princeton's women's center does run "moon groups" dedicated to the worship of pagan nature goddesses. Jan Strout, director of Princeton's women's center, defines this new feminist spirituality in these terms: "Part of what happens with patriarchy is this whole mind-body split, and it's sort of crazy-making. There's a desire to find a way of wholeness, a way of integration. We try to create new forms of woman-centered or nonhierarchical empowered notions of what it means to have a spiritual essence." Like other movements dealing in spiritual essence, this one is not immune to murky definitions of reality and truth.

To be a part of this blanket warmth, this woman-centered nonhierarchical empowered notion, students are willing to lie. My first year at Princeton, one student was caught fabricating a rape story. Mindy had spoken at Take Back the Night for each of her four years at Princeton, and she had printed her story in the *Daily Princetonian*. What's interesting is that her account didn't really stand out; she sounded like everyone else at the speak-out. Her story could have been the blueprint. Whatever else anyone can say about her, Mindy could really talk the talk.

Her story went like this: she left the eating clubs after one boy "started hitting on me in a way that made me feel particularly uncomfortable." He followed her home and "dragged" her back to his room. The entire campus, as she described it, was indifferent: "Although I screamed the entire time, no one called for help, no one even looked out the window to see if the person screaming was in danger." He "carried" her to his room "and, while he shouted the most degrading obscenities imaginable, raped me." He told her that "his father buys him cheap girls like me to use up and throw away." And then he banged her head against the metal bedpost until she was unconscious. She then explained that he was forced to leave campus for a year and now he was back. "Because I see this person every day," she claimed, "my rape remains a constant daily reality for me." Now, she said, she was on the road to recovery, and "there are some nights when I sleep soundly and there are even some mornings when I look in the mirror and I like what I see. I may be a victim, but now I am also a survivor."[7]

Unlike most participants in the speak-outs, Mindy put her story in print. Once it spilled over from the feverish midnight outpouring of the march into black-and-white newsprint, the facts could be checked. The problem was that she claimed she had reported a rape, and she hadn't. She claimed an administrator had told her "to let bygones be bygones," and he hadn't. She told people that a certain male undergraduate was the rapist, and he complained to the administration.

In May of her senior year, 1991, Mindy came clean. Responding to administrative pressure, she printed an apology for her false accusation in the *Daily Princetonian*. She wrote of the person she accused, "I have never met this individual or spoken to him . . . I urge students who are knowledgeable of this situation to cease blaming this person for my attack."[8] Mindy seemed to explain her motivation for inventing the story as political: "I made my statements in the *Daily Princetonian* and at the Take Back the Night March in order to raise awareness for the plight of the campus rape victims."[9] So these were fictions in the service of political truth.

Mindy also claimed that she was swept up in the heat of the moment. "In several personal conversations and especially at the Take Back the Night March, I have been overcome by emotion. As a result, I was not as coherent or accurate in my recounting of events as a situation as delicate as this demands." If Mindy's political zeal and emotional intensity blurred the truth of her story, one wonders how many other survivors experience a similar blurring.

The accusation is a serious one, and the boy Mindy accused was in a terrible position in the community until she set the record straight. Accusations of rape stick, and in the twisted justice of the grapevine no one is considered innocent until proven guilty. Some may say, as an editorial in the *Daily Princetonian* did, that Mindy's false accusation was "an isolated incident" and shouldn't affect anyone's attitude toward Take Back the Night. Others would go further and claim that the abstract truth in these accusations eclipses the literal falsehood. In a piece about William Kennedy Smith's date-rape trial, Catharine MacKinnon, a prominent feminist law professor, wrote that the truth of a given accusation should be weighed in the larger political balance: "Did this member of a group sexually trained to woman-hating aggression commit this particular act of woman-hating aggression?"[10] That people like MacKinnon are willing to sacrifice individual certainty to politicized group psychology only encourages the Mindys of the world to make up stories.

At George Washington University a few years ago, another student was caught inventing a rape. Mariam, a sophomore who worked in a rape-crisis center, told a story about "two muscular young-looking black males" in "torn dirty clothing" raping a white student. She later admitted to fabricating the story and wrote in a letter of apology that "my goal from the beginning was to call attention to what I perceived to be a serious safety concern for women."[11] As the black student organization at George Washington pointed out, the fabricated rape was not just a lie, but a lie promoting racist stereotypes.

The line between fact and fiction is a delicate one when it comes to survivor stories. In the heat of the moment, in the confessional rush of relating graphic details to a supportive crowd, the truth may be stretched, battered, or utterly abandoned. It's impossible to tell how many of these stories are authentic, faithful accounts of what actually happened. They all sound tinny, staged. Each "I am a survivor and I am here to take back the night" seems rehearsed. The context — microphone, hundreds of strangers, applause — puts what one survivor called "deepest darkest secrets" under a voyeuristic spotlight. As they listen to the stories, people cry and hold hands and put their arms around each other. The few moments before someone steps up to the microphone are thick with tension.

As students throw stories of suffering to the waiting crowds, the spiritual cleansing takes on darker undercurrents. The undercurrent is the competition for whose stories can be more Sadean, more incest-ridden, more violent, more like a paperback you can buy at a train station.

Under Blair Arch, a blind girl takes the microphone and says, I have been oppressed by everybody, straights and gays, Catholics, Jews and Protestants. Unless I am imagining it, a ripple of unease runs through the crowd. There is something obscene about this spectacle. This is theater, late-night drama. One earnest male Princeton junior tells me "it was better last year. More moving. There was more crying. Everyone was crying."

Some of these stories may be moving, may be heartfelt and true, but there is something about this context that numbs. Once, over a cup of coffee, a friend told me she had been raped by a stranger with a knife. I was startled. Small, neat, self-contained, she was not someone prone to bursts of self-revelation. She described it, the flash of the knife, the scramble, the exhaustion, the decision to keep her mind blank, the bruises and the police. After she had finished, she quickly resumed her competent, business-as-usual attitude, her toughness, but I could tell how hard it had been for her to tell me. I felt terrible for her. I felt like there was nothing I could say.

But an individual conversation is worlds away from the spectacle of mass confession. I find the public demand — and it is a demand — for intimacy strange and unconvincing. Public confidences have a peculiarly aggressive quality. As Wendy Kaminer writes in her book about the recovery movement, "Never have so many known so much about people for whom they cared so little."[12]

Besides the shady element of spectacle, the march itself is headed in the wrong direction. Take Back the Night works against its own political purpose. Although the

43

march is intended to celebrate and bolster women's strength, it seems instead to celebrate their vulnerability. The marchers seem to accept, even embrace, the mantle of victim status. As the speakers describe every fear, every possible horror suffered at the hands of men, the image they project is one of helplessness and passivity. The march elaborates on just how vulnerable women are. Someone tells me that she wanted to say to the male speaker who said "This isn't . . . a good night to be a man" that it wasn't such a good night to be a woman either. *Drained, beleaguered, anxious,* and *vulnerable* are the words women use to describe how they feel as they walk away from the march. But there is a reason they come year after year. There is power to be drawn from declaring one's victimhood and oppression. There is strength in numbers, and unfortunately right now there is strength in being the most oppressed. Students scramble for that microphone, for a chance for a moment of authority. But I wonder if this kind of authority, the coat-tugging authority of the downtrodden, is really worth it.

Betty Friedan stirred up controversy with a bold critique of the rape-crisis movement. She attacked the political efficacy of this victimized and victimizing stance when she wrote, "Obsession with rape, even offering Band-Aids to its victims, is a kind of wallowing in that victim state, that impotent rage, that sterile polarization."[13] *Impotent* and *sterile* are the right words. This is a dead-end gesture. Proclaiming victimhood doesn't help project strength.

44

Many of the Princeton students who take the microphone emanate a sense of entitlement. These students say, again and again, "It's not fair that I should be afraid." This is an idea that springs from privilege. Who besides these well-dressed, well-fed, well-groomed students would expect the right to safety and march for it? Many of these girls came to Princeton from Milton and Exeter. Many of their lives have been full of summers in Nantucket and horseback-riding lessons. These are women who have grown up expecting fairness, consideration, and politeness. They have grown up expecting security. Considering how many things there are to be afraid of and how many things are not fair, being frightened to walk around Princeton, New Jersey, late at night does not seem like one of God's greatest injustices.

Princeton is after all a pretty safe place, a quiet town. There's not much else besides a Laura Ashley and an ice cream store. And, for such a sleepy town, Princeton has a lot of police. Sometimes they stand outside the cash machine watching high school students watch each other. Once a policeman gave me a citation for jaywalking. Another time, at the train station, a tall, rangy old drunk started mumbling and shouting to himself. Within five minutes three policemen came to chase him away. All of this is to say that the Princeton police are not exactly busy combating violent crime. Myself, when I used to walk over the golf course to the graduate college, I was more afraid of wild geese than rapists.

Take Back the Night is an umbrella march covering fear in general, frustration in general, and the belief that men are out to get women in general. In the late seventies, at an early Take Back the Night march, Andrea Dworkin had these words to offer the gathering crowd:

> Men use the night to erase us. . . . The annihilation of a woman's personality, individuality, will, character, is prerequisite to male sexuality, and so the night is the sacred time of male sexual celebration, because it is dark and in the dark it is easier not to see: not to see who she is. Male sexuality, drunk on its intrinsic contempt for all life, but especially for women's lives, can run wild, hunt down random victims, use the dark for cover, find in the dark solace, sanctuary, cover.[14]

With her mystical fear, her barely suppressed hysteria, her baroque idiom, Andrea Dworkin captures something of the spirit of the night. Her vampire model of male sexuality captures the dramatic, paranoid edge of the march. Her rhetoric emphasizes how close the marchers come to the border of mystical fear. With candles and drumbeats, the image the marchers project is a fainter version of Dworkin's bold strokes. Few can summon up Dworkin's fevered pitch, her vampire imagery, but the sentiment is there, diluted, palatable, draped in loose words like "patriarchy." The primal idea of women as hunted and men as hunters is there.

At an early march one participant told the *Daily Princetonian*, "A man is as free to walk around at night as he wants and I'm not. I don't have that freedom."[15] The problem with this sentiment is that no one has complete freedom to walk around at night. Freedom from fear is a mythical premise and a state of mind. No one has absolute immunity from freak perils and strangers in the dark.

Anyone can be attacked, and anyone can choose to ignore the risks. Actually, Princeton's campus security estimates that half of all assaults reported involve male victims. Between 1983 and 1992 only 2 rapes have been reported to campus security. At Harvard in 1992, out of the 29 instances of assault and battery reported to campus police, 21 of the victims were male and 8 were female. Out of the 19 assaults with a deadly weapon reported, 16 victims were male and 3 were female. In addition, one sexual assault was reported to the Harvard police. Rape may be underreported, but these figures show that men are not immune to violent crime. According to these statistics a man walking home in Cambridge is more likely to be attacked than a woman.

Of course, men represent only a tiny percentage of victims of stranger rapes, but rape is much less common than other forms of assault. When I was living in New York, I knew lots of men who had been attacked, and fewer women. Numbers don't necessarily reflect anxiety levels. They don't necessarily reflect who feels more threatened by a dark alley and an empty lobby. But the numbers do show that everyone is at risk. The idea that men are safe and women are not, that danger is a gender issue, springs from something other than fact. Fear is not exclusively female. Although Andrea Dworkin doesn't seem to think so, Little Red Riding Hood is just a fairy tale, and whatever big bad wolves are out there are out to get all of us, flesh and blood, male or female. All of us are vulnerable to knife and gun, to drug-mad fiends. Men don't really use the night "to erase us," and we are not so easily erased.

Whatever else one can say about Take Back the Night, it is definitely filling a need. There is something pulling all of these students away from their computers and books, their parties and movies. In a decade and a half noted for political apathy, this is an issue that consistently attracts large numbers of students each year. In the past years at Princeton, each Take Back the Night march has drawn from five hundred to one thousand participants. Columbia's 1992 speak-outs lasted from nine at night until nine in the morning. In 1991, Bard College students took over a campus building to protest the administration's handling of sexual-assault cases.[16] At Stanford, the student government voted to spend forty-five thousand dollars of its own money for sexual-assault-prevention programs.[17] In a demonstration against the decision to acquit three male students of rape charges, students at the University of New Hampshire were arrested for occupying an administration building for four days.[18] Even at Princeton's conservative campus, there was a sit-in in 1990 to demand the addition of a full-time position for SHARE.

The marchers at Take Back the Night are not the

fringes; they are not the radical few. On some campuses even representatives of the administration march. At Princeton, in 1988, the university's president, a provost, and the dean of students marched. Professors sometimes march. The marches are not the production of one vocal clique. The students involved represent a cross section of the college community. At Princeton the march is sponsored by organizations ranging from the women's center to the dean of students to the women's lacrosse team.

Marjorie Metsch, the director of Columbia's peer-education program, points out that "Take Back the Night is one of the only consistent political activities that take place on this campus. It is unique in that it crosses over political lines, so that when you're marching you know that you're marching with women who probably would disagree with three quarters of what you say most of the time. Or you would never know them on the campus. But in that moment, in that time and in that space when you're all chanting and screaming and yelling and walking down the street, you're united in this issue."

An issue that unites such disparate elements, that compels so many students to act, demands scrutiny. Every spring, Take Back the Night marches crop up across the country. Each campus has a slightly different format, a slightly different emphasis, but they are all marching to the beat of the same drum.

Take Back the Night is becoming one of our society's coming-of-age rituals. Behind the speak-outs and the chants of "Women unite, take back the night" is something vivid against the drab political backdrop. I remember, when I was in college, looking out my window at the sea of faces, being perplexed, annoyed, uninterested. But now as the chants get louder, the speak-outs more lurid, I have begun to think that it's time to listen — not to what the marchers are saying, but to why.

The Rape Crisis, or
"Is Dating Dangerous?"

Radical feminists aren't the only ones talking about the rape crisis anymore. Since the mideighties the media have been kindling public interest in rape with a series of alarming revelations. In 1985, *Ms.* magazine published the startling results of an early study on rape in universities in a story dramatically entitled "Date Rape: The Story of an Epidemic and Those Who Deny It."[1] That same year, the *New York Times* ran an article called "A New Recognition of the Realities of 'Date Rape.'"[2] After William Kennedy Smith's televised date-rape trial, in 1991, there was a flurry of articles and editorials about rape. As everyone waited to see what would happen to the Kennedy name and his word against hers, a new discussion of the rape crisis opened up on the front pages, capturing public attention.

According to the widely quoted *Ms.* survey, one in four college women is the victim of rape or attempted rape. One in four. I remember standing outside the dining hall in college looking at a purple poster with this statistic written in bold letters. It didn't seem right. If sexual assault was really so pervasive, it seemed strange that the intricate gossip networks hadn't picked up more than one or two shadowy instances of rape. If I was really standing in the middle of an epidemic, a crisis, if 25 percent of my female friends were really being raped, wouldn't I know it? The answer is not that there is a conspiracy of silence. The answer is that measuring rape is not as straightforward as it seems.

Neil Gilbert, professor of social welfare at the University of California at Berkeley, has written several articles attacking the two sociological studies that are cornerstones of the rape-crisis movement, the *Ms.* magazine study and one done in the early eighties by Diana Russell. Having taken a closer look at the numbers, he questions the validity of the one-in-four statistic. He points out that in the *Ms.* study, which is the one most frequently quoted, 73 percent of the women categorized as rape victims did not define their experience as "rape."[3] It was Dr. Mary Koss, the psychologist conducting the study, who did. These are not self-proclaimed victims, then — these are victims according to someone else. From Koss's point of view, these women were suffering from what they used to call false consciousness. The way it is usually and tactfully phrased these days is that they don't recognize what has really happened to them.

Gilbert also points out that 42 percent of the women identified in this study as rape victims later had sex with the man who supposedly raped them *after* the supposed rape.[4] As Gilbert delves further into the numbers, he does not necessarily disprove the one-in-four statistic, but he does help clarify what it means. He reveals that the so-called "rape epidemic" on campuses is more a way of interpreting, a way of seeing, than a physical phenomenon. It is more about a change in sexual politics than a change in sexual behavior.

According to Gilbert, in the *Ms.* study one of the questions used to define rape was "Have you had sexual intercourse when you didn't want to because a man gave you alcohol or drugs?"[5] The strange phrasing of this question itself raises the issue of agency. Why aren't college women responsible for their own intake of alcohol or drugs? A man may *give* a woman drugs, but she herself decides to take them. A pamphlet about acquaintance rape gives the following as an example of a rape scenario: "A woman is at a party and is very drunk. A man, whom she knows through a friend, has had a few drinks with her. He leads her into an unoccupied room in the house. They begin to make out and he feels as if she is responding to him. They have intercourse. He leaves her in the room, asleep or passed out, and returns to the party."[6]

The idea is that women get too drunk to know what they are doing, while men stay sober and lucid. If we assume women are not all helpless and naive, then shouldn't they be held responsible for their choice to drink or take drugs? If a woman's judgment is impaired, as they say, and she has sex, it isn't necessarily always the man's fault; it isn't necessarily always rape. Many of these instances, as Gilbert points out, are simply too vague for statistical certainty. Classifying a positive answer to Koss's ambiguous question as rape further explains how she could have reached the conclusion that one in four women on college campuses has been raped.

As Gilbert points out, at Berkeley, a campus with 14,000 female students, only 2 rapes were reported to the police in 1990, and between 40 and 80 students sought assistance from the campus rape-counseling service. Even if we assume that many students don't report rapes, even to the sympathetic rape-crisis center, the one-in-four statistic would still leave thousands of rapes unaccounted for.

No matter how one feels about Gilbert's perspective, his research shows that these figures are subjective, that what is being called rape is not a clear-cut issue of common sense. Whether or not one in four college women has been raped, then, is a matter of opinion, not a matter of mathematical fact. Everyone agrees that rape is a terrible thing, but we don't agree on what rape is. There is a gray area in which someone's rape may be another person's bad night. Definitions become entangled in passionate ideological battles. There hasn't been a remarkable change in the number of women being raped, it seems, just a change in how receptive the political climate is to those numbers. As Koss herself phrased it, "In the past these cases would not have

54

come to light. But today more women are willing to recognize that the problem exists."[7] Clearly, from her perspective not enough women are "recognizing" the problem, since most of the women in her own study didn't recognize that, by Koss's standards, they had been raped.

The next questions, then, are who is identifying this epidemic and why. Somebody is "finding" this rape crisis, and finding it for a reason. Asserting the prevalence of rape lends urgency, authority, to a broader critique of culture. In a dramatic description of the rape crisis, Naomi Wolf writes in *The Beauty Myth,* "Cultural representation of glamorized degradation has created a situation among the young in which boys rape and girls get raped as *a normal course of events* [Wolf's italics]."[8] Whether or not she really believes rape is part of the "normal course of events" these days, Wolf is making a larger point. She is talking about the whole cultural climate surrounding sex. Wolf's rhetorical excess serves her polemic about sexual politics. Her dramatic prose is a call to arms. She is trying to rally the feminist troops. Wolf uses rape as a red flag, an undeniable sign that things are falling apart.

Back in 1975, Susan Brownmiller's best-selling, encyclopedic discussion of rape, *Against Our Will: Men, Women and Rape,* carried the issue into the mainstream. Brownmiller writes that "from prehistoric times to the present, I believe, rape has played a critical function. It is nothing more or less than a conscious process of intimidation by which *all men* keep *all women* in a state of fear

[Brownmiller's italics]."⁹ As Brownmiller's argument demonstrates, discussions of rape often extend beyond discussions of a physical act. With her grand, sometimes paranoid strokes, Brownmiller portrays rape as the central mechanism of oppression. She is describing rape as something originary, something that defines relations between men and women.

From Susan Brownmiller to Naomi Wolf, feminist prophets of the rape crisis are talking about something more than forced penetration. They are talking about rape as part of what is often referred to as "rape culture." Even a commonly circulated pamphlet about acquaintance rape giving practical advice includes this overtly ideological statement: "The images we see in advertisements, on television, and in movies portray forced sex as somehow natural and permissible, especially if it involves two people who know each other. These images reflect society's tolerance of acquaintance rape — an epidemic of violent crime."¹⁰ Even in the most pragmatic of contexts, numbers are marshaled behind a cause, and statistics about rape become more than just statistics about rape.

Rape is a natural trump card for feminism. Arguments about rape can be used to sequester feminism in the teary province of trauma and crisis. They can block analysis with statements like "You can't possibly understand what I've been through." Declarations of rape are used as an insurmountable obstacle, a point beyond which no questions are allowed.

Invoking the rape crisis, as Wolf and Brownmiller do, strengthens an argument by infusing it with heightened emotional appeal. For many feminists, then, rape becomes a vehicle, a way to get from here to there. By blocking analysis with its claims to unique pandemic suffering, the rape crisis becomes a powerful source of authority.

The idea of a rape epidemic has swollen beyond a few polemical passages. Although the rhetoric and statistics may be the stuff of airy political visions, they also affect real students and real financial decisions on college campuses. Universities channel money and resources, rooms, energy, and ideas into rape-counseling and education programs.

The fear of rape is not confined to university officials. It is not the kind of administrative worry that barely catches the attention of the average freshman. Students shout about it at Take Back the Night marches. They talk about it over coffee. At a party, standing in the corner, one can hear two college sophomores talking about the danger of being raped by friends. One of them says a male friend of hers recently confessed that he was infatuated with her. Afterward, she let him drive her home, she trusted him. Nothing happened, thank God, she tells her friend over her plastic cup of red punch, but it scares me to think of what could have, it scares me to think that I trusted him after I knew how he felt about me. Yeah, the other one agrees, you have to stay in public places in situations like that.

Dead serious, eyes wide with concern, one college

senior tells me that she believes one in four is too conservative an estimate. This is not the first time I've heard this.
She tells me the right statistic is closer to one in two. That
means one in two women is raped. It's amazing, she says,
amazing that so many of us are sexually assaulted every
day.

What is amazing is that this student actually believes
50 percent of women are raped. This is the true crisis: that
there are a not insignificant number of young women
walking around with this alarming belief. This hyperbole
contains within it a state of perpetual fear. A young woman
asks a male friend to walk her three blocks back to her
dorm at eight o'clock in the evening. Half of all women are
raped in their lifetime, and she cannot walk outside at
night without that thought hovering in the windblown
leaves, the shadowy corners, the empty cars. She says she is
glad they have those blue lights all over campus, although,
she adds grimly, they may not do any good — this is the
chorus of the rape crisis. And we certainly are in a state of
crisis if these college students really believe, as they walk
around, as they go to parties and lectures and late-night
movies, that they have a 50 percent chance of being raped.

"Acquaintance Rape: Is Dating Dangerous?" — a
pamphlet commonly found at counseling centers — gives a
sample date-rape scenario. On the cover, the title rises from
the shards of a shattered photograph of a boy and girl
dancing. The pamphlet tells us what "she" is thinking and
what "he" is thinking as the date progresses. She thinks:

"He was really handsome and he had a great smile. We talked and found we had a lot in common. When he asked me over to his place for a drink I thought it would be OK. He was such a good listener and I wanted him to ask me out again." She's just looking for a sensitive boy, a good listener with a great smile, but unfortunately his intentions are not as pure as hers.

Beneath his great smile, he is thinking: "She looked really hot, wearing a sexy dress that showed off her great body." They start talking right away. He knows that she likes him because she keeps smiling and touching his arm while she's speaking. He notes, "She seemed pretty relaxed so I asked her back to my place for a drink . . . when she said 'yes' I knew that I was going to be lucky."

When they get to his room the bed turns out to be the only place to sit. Our innocent heroine thinks, "I didn't want him to get the wrong idea but what else could I do?" They talk for a while and then he makes his move. She is startled. He begins by kissing. She says she really liked him so the kissing was nice. But then he pushes her down on the bed. She tries to get up and tells him to stop, but "he was so much bigger and stronger."[11]

These cardboard stereotypes are not just educating freshmen about rape, they are also educating them about "dates" and about sexual desire. With titles like "Friends Raping Friends: Could It Happen to You?" date-rape pamphlets call into question all relationships between men and women. Beyond just warning students about rape, this movement produces its own images of sexual behavior, in which men exert pressure and women resist. By defining the dangerous date in these terms — with this type of male and this type of female, and their different types of expectations — these pamphlets promote their own perspective on how men and women feel about sex: men are lascivious, women are innocent.

Although it is not always an explicit part of their agenda, feminists involved in the rape-crisis movement educate young women according to certain beliefs about sexual behavior, both real and ideal. The sleek images of pressure and resistance projected in movies, videotapes, pamphlets, and speeches create their own model of what is acceptable sexual behavior. The don'ts imply their own set of do's. The movement against rape, then, not only dictates the way sex *shouldn't be* but also the way it *should be*. Sex should be gentle, it should not be aggressive; it should be absolutely equal, it should not involve domination and submission; it should be tender, not ambivalent; it should communicate respect, not consuming desire.

In her book *Real Rape,* Susan Estrich, University of Southern California Law Center professor and formerly manager of Michael Dukakis's presidential campaign, slips her ideas about the nature of sexual encounters into her legal analysis of the problem. She writes,

> Many feminists would argue that so long as women are powerless relative to men, viewing a "yes" as a sign of true consent is misguided. For myself, I am quite certain that

many women who say yes to men they know, whether on dates or on the job, would say no if they could. I have no doubt that women's silence sometimes is not the product of passion and desire but of pressure and fear.[12]

Estrich's understanding of "real rape" springs, in part, from her understanding of "real" sex. Like Estrich, most rape-crisis feminists claim that they are not talking about sex, they're talking about violence. But, like Estrich, they are also talking about sex. With their practical advice, their sample scenarios, their sample aggressive male, their message itself projects a clear comment on the nature of sexuality: women are often unwilling participants who say yes because they feel they have to, because they are intimidated by male power.

Feminist definitions of rape do not exist in a realm completely separate from the law. In 1992 New Jersey's Supreme Court upheld its far-reaching rape laws. Ruling against a teenager charged with raping his date, the court concluded that signs of force or the threat of force is not necessary to prove the crime of rape — no force, that is, beyond that required for the physical act of penetration. Both the plaintiff and the defendant admitted that they were sexually involved, but the two sides differed on whether what happened that night was rape. It's hard to define anything that happens in that strange, libidinous province of adolescence, but this court upheld the judgment that the girl was raped. If the defendant had been an adult he could have gone to jail for up to ten years. Susan

Herman, deputy public defender in the case, remarked, "You not only have to bring a condom on a date, you have to bring a consent form as well."[13]

The idea of consent has gone beyond the simple assertion that no means no. Politically correct sex involves a yes, and a specific yes at that: a new standard pamphlet on acquaintance rape warns men that "hearing a clear sober 'yes' to the question 'Do you want to make love?' is very different from thinking, 'Well, she didn't say no.' "[14] The yes must be clear, the yes must be sober. The idea of explicit permission has crept into rape-crisis feminism and into the standard literature on the subject.[15]

According to the premise of active consent, we can no longer afford ambiguity. We can no longer afford the dangers of unspoken consent. A former director of Columbia's date-rape education program told *New York* magazine, "Every time you have intercourse there must be explicit consent, and if there's no explicit consent then it's rape. . . . Stone silence throughout a physical encounter with someone is not explicit consent."[16] This apparently practical, apparently clinical proscription cloaks retrograde assumptions about the way men and women experience sex. The idea that only an explicit yes means yes proposes that women, like children, have trouble communicating what they want. It proposes that words are likely to escape us, that we are likely to find ourselves tangled in situations where we can't assert our desires. Beyond its dubious premises about the limits of female communication, the idea of active consent bolsters stereotypes of men just out to "get some" and women who don't really want any.

The American College Health Association's pamphlet tells men: "Your desires may be beyond your control, but your actions are within your control." And it warns the female student to "communicate your limits clearly." According to this picture of sexual relations, her desires are never beyond her control. The assumption embedded in the movement against date rape is our grandmothers' assumption: men want sex, women don't. In emphasizing this struggle — he pushing, she resisting — the rape-crisis movement recycles and promotes an old model of sexuality.

In her recent book, *Feminism Without Illusions,* Elizabeth Fox-Genovese describes the "epidemic" in these terms:

> Although the sexual revolution has "liberated" young women from many of the older constraints of propriety, it has also deprived them of the attendant protections. . . . [They] have cause to worry that when they choose not to have sexual relations with a particular man, their "no" may not be respected. The ensuing confusion has given rise to the epidemic of "acquaintance rape" on campuses.[17]

Fox-Genovese's analysis is tinged with regret. She notes that along with freedom comes risk. Broken taboos are broken locks: they leave female experience open to new dangers.

Robin Warshaw, in *I Never Called It Rape,* expresses her nostalgia for days of greater social control:

Up until the 1970s, colleges adopted a "substitute parent" attitude toward their students, complete with curfews (often more strict for females than males), liquor bans, and stringent disciplinary punishments. In that era, students were punished for violating the three-feet-on-the-floor rules during coed visiting hours in dormitories or being caught with alcohol on school property. Although those regulations did not prevent acquaintance rape, they undoubtedly kept down the numbers of incidents by making women's dorms havens of no-men-allowed safety.[18]

While sequestering women in "havens of no-men-allowed safety" may seem undesirable to most of us, later in her book Warshaw recommends creating single-sex dorms and redesigning coed dorms to separate the sexes more effectively.[19] Her recommendations push college life back into the fifties. William Bennett, Ronald Reagan's conservative secretary of education, also pushed for the university to act "in loco parentis." He called for universities to not stay neutral in the choice between "decent morality and decadence."[20] The rhetoric of feminists and conservatives blurs and overlaps in this desire to keep our youth safe and pure.

One book, *Avoiding Rape On and Off Campus,* by Carol Pritchard, warns young women to "think carefully before you go to a male friend's apartment or dorm. . . . Do not expose yourself to any unnecessary risk." In formulating this advice, Pritchard expresses a worldview in which danger obscures sexuality, in which the prospect of what happens between male and female friends in a private room becomes "unnecessary risk." We must be fragile creatures if we need such an extreme definition of safety.

Another commonly distributed pamphlet about rape advises young women, "Since you may not know who has the potential for rape, be on your guard with every man." This is another way of phrasing Susan Brownmiller's clever warning that "the typical American rapist might be the boy next door."[21] Such literature states that no man should be immune from suspicion. A book about rape issues the radical, myth-breaking warning that " 'nice' men do rape, and they do rape 'nice' women."[22] All of this suggests that we should subject all of our male friends to scrutiny, because, after all, men want one thing and one thing only.

The "Is Dating Dangerous?" pamphlet, and the others of its ilk, are clearly designed to protect innocent college women from the insatiable force of male desire. This is the old sugar-and-spice approach to female character. We have been hearing about this for centuries. He is still nearly uncontrollable; she is still the one drawing lines. In HBO's drama about date rape, *The Katie Koestner Story*, the date-rape victim, Katie, is a virgin who sleeps with a stuffed animal in her bed. This is not an arbitrary characterization: the portrait of innocence defiled, Katie is the standard representation of a date-rape victim. Again and again, the rape-crisis movement peddles images of gender relations that deny female desire and infantilize women. Once again our bodies seem to be sacred vessels. We've come a long way, and now it seems we are going back.

Some date-rape pamphlets have actually begun to sound like Victorian guides to conduct. The American College Health Association pamphlet advises its delicate reader that "if someone starts to offend you, tell them firmly and early."[23] Sharing these assumptions, *The Young Lady's Friend,* a manners guide from 1857, counsels young women,

> Never join in any rude plays, that will subject you to being kissed or handled in any way by gentlemen. Do not suffer your hand to be held or squeezed without showing it displeases you by instantly withdrawing it ... sit not with another in a place that is too narrow; read not out of the same book; let not your eagerness to see anything induce you to place your head close to another person's. These, and many other little points of delicacy and refinement, deserve to be made fixed habits, and then they will sit easily and gracefully upon you, heightening the respect of all who approach you, and operating as an almost invisible though a very impenetrable fence, keeping off the vulgar familiarity and that desecration of the person that has so often led to vice.[24]

By viewing rape as encompassing more than the use or threat of physical violence to coerce someone into sex, rape-crisis feminists reinforce traditional views about the fragility of the female body and will. Today's definition of date or acquaintance rape stretches beyond acts of violence or physical force. According to common definitions of date rape, even verbal coercion or manipulation constitutes rape. Verbal coercion is defined as "a woman's consenting to unwanted sexual activity because of a man's verbal arguments not including verbal threats of force."[25] The belief that verbal coercion is rape extends beyond official definitions; it pervades workshops, counseling sessions, and student opinion pieces. In Harvard's moderate feminist magazine, the *Lighthouse,* a student wrote an impassioned piece about the prevalence of what she considered emotional rape.

In an essay entitled "Nonviolent Sexual Coercion," psychologists Charlene Muelenhard and Jennifer Schrag include the remarks "He said he'd break up with me if I didn't," "He said I was frigid," and "He said everyone's doing it" in the category of verbal coercion. They go on to explain that "a woman with low self-esteem might feel that if she refuses her partner's sexual advances she will lose him, and her value will be lessened because she is no longer associated with him."[26] This is a portrait of the cowering woman, knocked on her back by the barest feather of peer pressure. Solidifying this image of women into policy implies an acceptance of the passive role. By protecting women against verbal coercion, these feminists are promoting the view of women as weak-willed, alabaster bodies, whose virtue must be protected from the cunning encroachments of the outside world. The idea that women can't withstand verbal or emotional pressure infantilizes them. The suggestion lurking beneath this definition of rape is that men are not just physically but intellectually and emotionally more powerful than women. Printing pamphlets about verbal coercion institutionalizes an unacceptable female position.

We should not nurture this woman on her back, her will so mutable, so easily shaped; we should not support her in her passivity. We are not this woman on her back. We do not have the mind of an eleven-year-old in the body of a twenty-year-old. All competent female college students are compromised by the association of gullibility, low self-esteem, and the inability to assert ourselves with our position in relation to men. We should not be pressured and intimidated by words like "I'll break up with you if you don't" — and anyone who is intimidated should be recognized as the exception, not the rule. Allowing verbal coercion to constitute rape is a sign of tolerance toward the ultrafeminine stance of passivity. The brand of "low self-esteem" these psychologists describe should not be tolerated, it should be changed. Whether or not we feel pressured, regardless of our level of self-esteem, the responsibility for our actions is still our own.

Imagine men sitting around in a circle talking about how she called him impotent and how she manipulated him into sex, how violated and dirty he felt afterward, how coercive she was, how she got him drunk first, how he hated his body and couldn't eat for three weeks afterward. Imagine him calling this rape. Everyone feels the weight of emotional pressure at one time or another. The question is not whether people pressure each other, but how that pressure is transformed in our mind and culture into full-blown assault. There would never be a rule or a law, or even a pamphlet or peer-counseling group, for men who claimed to have been emotionally raped or verbally pressured into sex. And for the same reasons — assumptions of basic competence, free will, and strength of character — there should be no such rules or groups or pamphlets for women.

A manners guide from 1848 warns young women about the perils of verbally coercive men:

> The more attractive his exterior, the more dangerous he is as a companion for a young and inexperienced girl, and the more likely to dazzle and bewilder her mind. . . . He can with a subtlety almost beyond the power of her detection, change her ordinary views of things, confuse her judgements, and destroy her rational confidence in discriminating the powers of her own mind.[27]

The fear of verbal coercion, then, does not have its origins in modern feminism. The idea that young girls will be swayed, their judgment overturned, their mind dazzled and bewildered, by the sheer force of masculine logic has been included in date-rape pamphlets for more than a century.

Any value there may be in promoting this idea about female passivity and gullibility is eclipsed by its negative effects. Feminist educators should keep track of the images they project: women can't take care of themselves, they can't make their own decisions with a clear head.

In discussing rape, campus feminists often slip into an outdated, sexist vocabulary. "Rape" is a dangerous word. As Susan Sontag has warned us about illness, we have to be careful of rape as metaphor. The sheer physical fact of rape has always been loaded with cultural meaning. Throughout history, women's bodies have been seen as property, as chaste objects, as virtuous vessels to be "dishonored," "ruined," "defiled." Their purity or lack of purity has been a measure of value for the men to whom they belonged.

Shakespeare's Lucrece is "spotted, spoiled, corrupted" after her rape.[28] The tragic dimensions of Lucrece's personal trauma have more to do with conceptions of honor, virtue, and chastity than her own visceral experience. Lucrece worries about the shadow the rape will cast on her husband's reputation. Shakespeare's Titus Andronicus kills his daughter after she has been raped. Her virtue was so important, so vital, that once she was ravished, her life was worth nothing. Rape-crisis feminists reproduce the idea that there is something vulnerable to be taken or lost, that there is something pure to be violated.

"Politically, I call it rape whenever a woman has sex and feels violated," writes Catharine MacKinnon.[29] The language of virtue and violation reinforces stereotypes. It backs women into old corners. Younger feminists share MacKinnon's vocabulary and the accompanying assumptions about women's bodies. In one student's account of date rape in the *Rag*, she talks about the anguish of being "defiled."[30] Another student writes of her feelings after being raped, "I long to be innocent again."[31] With such anachronistic constructions of the female body, with all their assumptions about female purity, these young women frame their experience of rape in archaic, sexist terms.

Combating myths about rape is one of the central missions of the leaders of the rape-crisis movement. They spend money and energy trying to break down myths like "She asked for it." But with all their noise about rape myths, rape-crisis feminists are generating their own. If you look at the scenes described in the plays, the poems, the pamphlets, the Take Back the Night speak-outs, the stories told are loss-of-innocence stories. We all know this plot: I trusted him — I thought people were good — then I realized — afterward I knew. The rape, or sexual assault, is the moment of the fall. It is the isolated instant when, in one victim's words, they "learn to hate."

Take Back the Night marches are propelled by this myth of innocence lost. All the talk about empowering the voiceless dissolves into the image of the naive girl child who trusts the rakish man. This is a plot that reaches back centuries. It is the plot that propels Samuel Richardson's eighteenth-century epistolary novel *Clarissa*. After hundreds of pages chronicling the minute details of her plight, her seduction and resistance, her break from her family, Clarissa is raped by the duplicitous Robert Lovelace. Afterward she refuses to eat and fades toward a very virtuous, very religious death. Her coffin is finally returned to her father's house. More than a thousand pages are devoted to the story of her fall from innocence, a weighty event by eighteenth-century standards. But did these twentieth-century girls, raised on Madonna videos and the six o'clock news, really trust that people were good until they themselves were raped? Maybe. Were these girls, raised on horror movies and glossy Hollywood sex scenes, really as innocent as all that? Maybe. But maybe the myth of lost innocence is a trope — convenient, appealing, politically effective.

As long as we're taking back the night, we might as well take back our own purity. Sure, we were all kind of innocent, playing in the sandbox with bright red shovels, boys too. We can all look back through the tumultuous tunnel of adolescence on a honey-glazed childhood, with simple rules and early bedtimes. (We don't have to look at parents fighting, at sibling struggles, at casting out one best friend for another in the Darwinian playground — this is not the innocence lost, this is the innocence we never had.)

The idea of a fall from childhood grace, pinned on one particular moment — a moment over which we had no control, much lamented — gives our lives a compelling narrative structure. It's easy to see why the seventeen-year-old likes it. It's easy to see why the rape-crisis feminists like it. It's a natural human impulse put to political purpose. But in generating and perpetuating these kinds of myths we should keep in mind that myths surrounding female innocence have been used to keep women inside and behind veils. They have been used to keep them out of work and in labor.

In his book about crime written in 1886, police inspector Thomas Byrnes refers to rape as "a more fearful crime than murder."[32] With this telling description, he voices the belief that a woman's honor is more valuable than her life. The rape-crisis movement veers dangerously close to Byrnes's attitude about female bodies, with its expansive definitions of rape and implicit belief in the supremacy of the act of "violation" over other forms of violence.

Like the nineteenth-century police inspector, Andrea Dworkin blurs the line between rape and death. In a metaphor sweeping beyond rape, she writes, "The traditional flowers of courtship are the traditional flowers of the grave, delivered to the victim before the kill. The cadaver is dressed up and made up and laid down and ritually violated and consecrated to an eternity of being used."[33] She is talking about something more pervasive than the murder that sometimes accompanies violent rape. She is talking about what she sees as the "ritual violation" of all male-female relationships.

Rape-crisis feminists, even those less imaginative or excessive than Dworkin, reproduce the idea that guarding women's bodies from male violation is a life-or-death issue. To call date-rape victims "survivors," like survivors of a fire, a plane crash, or the Holocaust, is to compare rape to death. If date rape is as destructive as many feminists would have us believe, if women's lives really are *always* shattered by physically or emotionally forced sex, or intox-

icated sex, then perhaps rape does become a crime compa-
rable to murder.

Of course, sophisticated modern-day feminists don't
use words like "honor" or "virtue" anymore. They know
better than to say rape victims have been "defiled." Instead,
they call it posttraumatic stress syndrome. They tell the
victim she should not feel "shame," she should feel "trau-
matized." Within their overtly political psychology, forced
physical penetration takes on a level of metaphysical sig-
nificance: date rape resonates through a woman's entire
life. The idea that date rape remains with the victim, that it
necessarily cripples her, that she can never trust men again,
that she must be counseled, and angry that society has
done this to her, that rape culture and MTV and "glamorized images of degraded women" have done this to her,
are part and parcel of the same old ethos of female victimhood. In institutionalizing the assumption that rape is universally life-threatening, feminists are institutionalizing
female weakness.

Instead of rejecting the ideas about women's bodies
and chastity that go along with traditional conceptions of
rape, rape-crisis feminists are calling them by a new name.
It's not hard to imagine Clarissa, in jeans and a sweatshirt,
transported into the twentieth century, at a Take Back the
Night march. She would speak for a long time about her
deception and rape, about verbal coercion and anorexia,
about her ensuing posttraumatic stress syndrome. Latter-
day Clarissas may worry more about their self-esteem than

their virtue, but they are still attaching the same quasi-religious value to the physical act.

"Calling It Rape," a play written and conceived by a Harvard student, begins with a well-known poem from the seventeenth century, "To His Coy Mistress." Although generations of high school and college students have read this as a romantic poem, a poem about desire and the struggle against mortality, this play's author has reinterpreted it as a poem about rape. Andrew Marvell's speaker does indeed try to persuade the lady to come to bed. He dispenses with the traditional Petrarchan rhapsodies of praise and proclaims the urgency of his desire. "Had we but world enough, and time, / This coyness, lady, were no crime." But what Marvell didn't know then, and we know now, is that the real crime is not coyness, but persuasion. When he writes "Let us roll all our strength, and all / Our sweetness up into one ball; / And tear our pleasures with rough strife, / Through the iron gates of life," this is of course verbal coercion.

In the same play, the actors recount a rape that hinges on misunderstanding. The boy and girl are watching videos, and he starts to come on to her. The girl does not want to have sex. As the situation progresses, she says, in an oblique effort to communicate her lack of enthusiasm, "If you're going to fuck me use a condom." He interprets that as a yes, but it's really a no. And, according to this play, what happens next, condom or no condom, is rape.

This is one of the central ideas of the rape-crisis movement: sex has become our Tower of Babel. He doesn't know what she wants (not to have sex), and she doesn't know what he wants (to have sex), until it's too late. The idea is that he speaks boyspeak, and she speaks girlspeak, and what comes out of all this verbal chaos is a lot of rapes. More than a poststructuralist distrust of linguistic certainty, this is an idea about the mystery of the opposite sex. An idea about division, this is also a divisive idea. It promotes the image of men and women as inhabitants of different worlds. It raises the old-fashioned question Who can ever know what goes on in her pretty little head?

The theory of mixed signals and crossed stars has to do with more than gender politics. The idea of miscommunication, so central to the rape-crisis movement, is one piece of a larger social puzzle, and the idea that he may rape her because he doesn't know what she wants has its roots in more than male oblivion. This fear of miscommunication comes, in part, from the much-heralded diversity that has so radically shifted the social composition of the college class since the fifties.

Take my own college dorm: the Adams House dining hall is large, with high ceilings, dark wood tables, and portraits of the Adams family on the walls. It hasn't changed much for generations. The smoking section has grown and shrunk over the years, but the room looks the same. As soon as the students start milling around, gathering salads, ice cream, and coffee onto green trays, there are signs of change. There are students in jeans, flannel shirts, short skirts, girls in jackets, boys in bracelets, two pierced noses, and lots of secondhand clothes.

Not so long ago, this room was filled with boys in jackets and ties. They were all white, mostly Christian, and mostly what we now call privileged. Between quotas, legacies, and separate-sex colleges, students were more homogenized than milk. Diversity and multiculturalism hadn't been heard of, and if they had been, they would have been dirty words. The number of Jews was small. Separate schools then, Harvard and Radcliffe were almost entirely composed of boys and girls from the same background, the same dancing schools, prep schools, and sailing clubs. The shared culture was white Anglo-Saxon Protestant with money. Students came from the same social milieu with the same social rules, and it was assumed that everyone knew more or less how they were expected to behave with everyone else.

With the radical shift in college environment, with the introduction of black kids, Asian kids, Jewish kids, kids from the wrong side of the tracks of nearly every railroad in the country, there was an accompanying anxiety about how people were to behave. When ivory tower meets melting pot, it causes some confusion, some tension, some need for readjustment. In explaining the need for intensive "orientation" programs, including workshops on date rape, Columbia's assistant dean for freshmen stated, "You can't bring all these people together and say, 'Now be one big happy community,' without some sort of training. You can't just throw together somebody from a small town in Texas, and someone from New York City and someone from a conservative fundamentalist home in the Midwest and say 'Now without any sort of conversation be best friends and get along and respect one another.' "[34]

Some of the concern about date rape, then, springs from the juxtaposition of different cultures. As universities opened their doors wider, adults began to worry about what exactly those kids were doing behind those ivy-covered walls. "The campus is no longer a walled garden," declares one feminist discussion of sexual assault.[35]

Democracy is always messier than aristocracy. As fairness broke through the sacred boundaries of "our own kind," people worried. That worry, that social anxiety, is part of the concern about sexual harassment and concern about rape. Catherine Stimpson, feminist dean of Rutgers University and longtime advocate of women's-studies programs, once pointed out that it's easier for people to talk about gender than to talk about class. "Miscommunication" is in some sense a word for the friction between the way we were and the way we are. Just as the idea that we speak different languages is connected to gender — the arrival of women in classrooms, in dorms, and in offices — it is also connected to class.

When the southern heiress goes out with the plumber's son from the Bronx, when the kid from rural Arkansas goes out with a boy from Exeter, the anxiety is that they have different expectations. Concern with rape, with verbal coercion, is part class prejudice and race prejudice. The dangerous "miscommunication" that recurs through the literature on date rape is a code word for difference in background. The rhetoric surrounding date rape and sexual harassment is in part a response to cultural mixing, desirable as it seems in theory to the people who write college catalogs, and the idea that men don't know what women mean when women say no stems from something deeper and more complicated than feminist concerns with rape. The conservative thrust of the movement against date rape is that women need to be protected from men who don't share their social background.

People have asked me if I have ever been date-raped. And thinking back on complicated nights, on too many glasses of wine, on strange and familiar beds, I would have to say yes. With such a sweeping definition of rape, I wonder how many people there are, male or female, who haven't been date-raped at one point or another. People pressure and manipulate and cajole each other into all sorts of things all the time. As Susan Sontag writes, "Since Christianity upped the ante and concentrated on sexual behavior as the root of virtue, everything pertaining to sex has been a 'special case' in our culture, evoking peculiarly inconsistent attitudes."[36] No human interactions are free from pressure, and the idea that sex is, or can be, makes it what Sontag calls a "special case," vulnerable to the inconsistent expectations of double standard.

With their expansive version of rape, rape-crisis feminists invent a kinder, gentler sexuality. Beneath the broad definition of rape, these feminists are endorsing their own utopian vision of sexual relations: sex without struggle, sex without power, sex without persuasion, sex without pursuit. If verbal coercion constitutes rape, then the word "rape" itself expands to include any kind of sex a woman experiences as negative.

When the novelist Martin Amis spoke at Princeton in 1992, he included a controversial joke: "As far as I'm concerned you can change your mind before, even during, but just not after sex." The reason this joke is funny, and the reason it's also too serious to be funny, is that in the current atmosphere you *can* change your mind afterward. Regret can signify rape. A night that was a blur, a night you wish hadn't happened, can be rape. Since verbal coercion and manipulation are ambiguous, it's easy to decide afterward that he manipulated you. You can realize it weeks or even years later. A psychiatrist at a West Coast campus told me that when he was on call, a patient called him at three in the morning to say that she had just realized she'd been raped two years earlier. This kind of belated revelation is not uncommon. A pamphlet warns that "a friend who has been raped may confide in you 10 minutes or 10 years after the attack."[37] This is a movement that deals in retrospective trauma.

"Rape" becomes a catchall expression, a word used to define everything that is unpleasant and disturbing about relations between the sexes. Students say things like "I realize that sexual harassment is a kind of rape."[38] If we refer to a spectrum of behavior from emotional pressure to sexual harassment as rape, then the idea itself gets diluted. It ceases to be powerful as either description or accusation. We threaten to confirm the vision of that eighteenth-century patriarch Henry Fielding when he writes, "These words of exclamation, (murder!robbery!rape!) are used by ladies in a fright as fa la la da sa are in music only as vehicles of sound and without any fixed idea."[39]

On the not-so-distant edge of the spectrum, carrying this rhetoric to its logical conclusion, some feminists actually collapse the distinction between rape and sex. Catharine MacKinnon writes, "Compare victims' reports of rape with women's reports of sex. They look a lot alike. . . . In this light, the major distinction between intercourse (normal) and rape (abnormal) is that the normal happens so often that one cannot get anyone to see anything wrong with it."[40]

There are a few feminists involved in rape education who object to the current expanding definitions of sexual assault. Gillian Greensite, founder of the rape prevention education program at the University of Southern California at Santa Cruz, writes that the seriousness of the crime "is being undermined by the growing tendency of some feminists to label all heterosexual miscommunication and insensitivity as acquaintance rape."[41] From within the rape-crisis movement, Greensite's dissent makes an important point. If we are going to maintain an idea of rape, then

81

we need to reserve it for instances of physical violence or the threat of physical violence. One woman, raped by a stranger at knife point, says that although she feels bad for women raped by their former boyfriend, she does not think their experience should be equated with hers.

Going against the current of much rape-crisis feminism, Marjorie Metsch, Columbia's director of peer education, also distinguishes between rape and bad sex. "Most of the time when someone comes in and says 'I was really really drunk and I shouldn't have had sex last night,' it is not the same as saying 'I was raped.' My attitude is that you do not use language that the person herself is not using. It could be that it was just bad sex." Metsch reasons that the social and psychological weight of the word "rape" eclipses its descriptive value in cases of regretted sex. With this approach, she avoids injecting everyday college life with the melodrama of the rape crisis.

But some people want that melodrama. They want the absolute value placed on experience by absolute words. Words like "rape" and "verbal coercion" sculpt the confusing mass of experience into something easy to understand. The idea of date rape comes at us fast and coherent. It comes at us when we've just left home and haven't yet figured out where to put our new futon or how to organize our new social life. The rhetoric about date rape defines the terms, gives names to nameless confusions, and sorts through mixed feelings with a sort of insistent consistency. In the first rush of sexual experience, the fear of date rape offers a tangible framework in which to locate fears that are essentially abstract.

When my mother was young, navigating her way through dates, there was a definite social compass. There were places not to let him put his hands. There were invisible lines. The pill wasn't available, abortion wasn't legal, and sex was just wrong. Her mother gave her "mad money" to take out on dates in case her date got drunk and she needed to escape. She had to go far enough to hold his interest, and not far enough to endanger her reputation.

Now the rape-crisis feminists are offering new rules. They are giving a new political weight to the same old no. My mother's mother told her to drink sloe gin fizzes so she wouldn't drink too much and get too drunk and go too far. Now the date-rape pamphlets tell us, "Avoid excessive use of alcohol and drugs. Alcohol and drugs interfere with clear thinking and effective communication."[42]

My mother's mother told her to stay away from empty rooms and dimly lit streets. In her guidelines about rape prevention, Robin Warshaw writes, "Especially with a recent acquaintance, women should insist on going only to public places such as restaurants and movie theaters."[43]

There is a danger in these new rules. We shouldn't need to be reminded that the rigidly conformist fifties were not the heyday of women's power. Barbara Ehrenreich writes of "re-making love," but there is a danger in remaking love in its old image. While the terms may have changed, attitudes about sex and women's bodies have not.

83

Rape-crisis feminists threaten the progress that's been made. They are chasing the same stereotypes our mothers spent so much energy running away from.

One day I was looking through my mother's bookshelves, and I found her old, battered copy of Germaine Greer's feminist classic, *The Female Eunuch*. The pages were dog-eared, and whole passages were marked with penciled notes. It was 1971 when Germaine Greer fanned the fires with *The Female Eunuch*, and it was 1971 when my mother read it, brand-new, explosive, a tough and sexy terrorism for the early stirrings of the feminist movement.

Today's rape-crisis feminists threaten to create their own version of the desexualized woman Greer complained of twenty years ago. Her comments need to be recycled for present-day feminism. "It is often falsely assumed," Greer writes,

> even by feminists, that sexuality is the enemy of the female who really wants to develop these aspects of her personality. . . . It was not the insistence on her sex that weakened the American woman student's desire to make something of her education, but the insistence upon a *passive* sexual *role* [Greer's italics]. In fact, the chief instrument in the deflection and perversion of female energy is the denial of female sexuality for the substitution of femininity or sexlessness.[44]

It is the passive sexual role that threatens us still, and it is the denial of female sexual agency that threatens to propel us backward.

84

Reckless Eyeballing: Sexual Harassment on Campus

For generations, women have talked and written and theorized about their problems with men. But theories about patriarchy tumble from abstraction when you wake up next to it in the morning. Denouncing male oppression clashes with wanting him anyhow. From playgrounds to consciousness-raising groups, from suffragette marches to prochoice marches, women have been talking their way through this contradiction for a long time.

Sometimes my younger sister and I go out for coffee and talk about our relationships. We analyze everything: why he acts that way, how unfair this is, how we shouldn't be waiting for his call, and how we have better things to do with our time anyway. How men are always like that, and we are always like this, and our conversation goes on, endless, pleasurable, interesting, over many refills, until we go home and wait for their calls.

Heterosexual desire inevitably raises conflicts for the passionate feminist, and it's not an issue easily evaded. Sooner or later feminism has to address "the man question." But this is more than just a practical question of procreation, more than the well-worn translation of personal into political. It's also a question for the abstract, the ideological, the furthest reaches of the feminist imagination.

Charlotte Perkins Gilman, a prominent feminist writing at the turn of the century, found a fictional solution to the conflict between sex and feminism in her utopian novel, *Herland*. Her solution is simple: there is no sexual desire. Even after the male anthropologists arrive with their worldly lusts, the women of Herland remain unruffled. Everything runs smoothly and rationally in Herland, and through the entire course of the book none of the women harbors any sexual feelings, toward men or toward each other. They magically reproduce by parthenogenesis, and motherhood is their driving passion.

Gilman erases whatever problems arise from sexual involvements with men in her happy, if sterile, vision of clean streets, clean hearts, clean minds. In her sociological work, *Women and Economics,* Gilman applies the same device — obliterating the source of conflict — to another site of struggle. She conceives of houses without kitchens as the solution to women's household drudgery. The problem is that most people want kitchens, and most people want sex.

Many of today's feminists, in their focus on sexual harassment, share Gilman's sexual politics. In their videos, literature, and workshops, these feminists are creating their own utopian visions of human sexuality. They imagine a world where all expressions of sexual appreciation are appreciated. They imagine a totally symmetrical universe, where people aren't silly, rude, awkward, excessive, or confused. And if they are, they are violating the rules and are subject to disciplinary proceedings.

A Princeton pamphlet declares that "sexual harassment is unwanted sexual attention that makes a person feel uncomfortable or causes problems in school or at work, or in social settings."[1] The word "uncomfortable" echoes through all the literature on sexual harassment. The feminists concerned with this issue, then, propose the right to be comfortable as a feminist principle.

The difficulty with these rules is that, although it may infringe on the right to comfort, unwanted sexual attention is part of nature. To find wanted sexual attention, you have to give and receive a certain amount of unwanted sexual attention. Clearly, the truth is that if no one was ever allowed to risk offering unsolicited sexual attention, we would all be solitary creatures.

The category of sexual harassment, according to current campus definitions, is not confined to relationships involving power inequity. Echoing many other common definitions of sexual harassment, Princeton's pamphlet warns that "sexual harassment can occur between two people regardless of whether or not one has power over the other."[2] The weight of this definition of sexual harassment, then, falls on gender instead of status.[3]

In current definitions of sexual harassment, there is an implication that gender is so important that it eclipses all other forms of power. The driving idea behind these rules is that gender itself is a sufficient source of power to constitute sexual harassment. Catharine MacKinnon, an early theorist of sexual harassment, writes that "situations of co-equal power — among co-workers or students or teachers — are difficult to see as examples of sexual harassment unless you have a notion of male power. I think we lie to women when we call it not power when a woman is come on to by a man who is not her employer, not her teacher."[4] With this description, MacKinnon extends the province of male power beyond that of tangible social power. She proposes using the words "sexual harassment" as a way to name what she sees as a fundamental social and political inequity between men and women. Following in this line of thought, Elizabeth Grauerholz, a sociology professor, conducted a study about instances of male students harassing their female professors, a phenomenon she calls "contrapower harassment."[5]

Recently, at the University of Michigan, a female teaching assistant almost brought a male student up on charges of sexual harassment. She was offended by an example he used in a paper about polls — a few sentences about "Dave Stud" entertaining ladies in his apartment when he receives a call from a pollster — and she showed the paper to the professor of the class. He apparently encouraged her to see the offending example as an instance of sexual harassment. She decided not to press charges, although she warned the student that the next time anything else like this happened, in writing or in person, she would not hesitate. The student wisely dropped the course. To understand how this student's paragraph about Dave Stud might sexually harass his teacher, when he has much more to lose than she does, one must recognize the deeply sexist assumptions about male-female relations behind the teaching assistant's charge.

The idea that a male student can sexually harass a female professor, overturning social and institutional hierarchy, solely on the basis of some primal or socially conditioned male power over women is insulting. The mere fact of being a man doesn't give the male student so much power that he can plow through social hierarchies, grabbing what he wants, intimidating all the cowering female faculty in his path. The assumption that female students or faculty must be protected from the sexual harassment of male peers or inferiors promotes the regrettable idea that men are natively more powerful than women.

Even if you argue, as many do, that *in this society* men are simply much more powerful than women, this is still a dangerous train of thought. It carries us someplace we don't want to be. Rules and laws based on the premise that all women need protection from all men, because they are so much weaker, serve only to reinforce the image of women as powerless.

Our female professors and high-ranking executives, our congresswomen and editors, are every bit as strong as their male counterparts. They have earned their position of authority. To declare that their authority is vulnerable to a dirty joke from someone of inferior status just because that person happens to be a man is to undermine their position. Female authority is not (and should not be seen as) so fragile that it shatters at the first sign of male sexuality. Any rules saying otherwise strip women, in the public eye, of their hard-earned authority.

Since common definitions of sexual harassment include harassment between peers, the emphasis is not on external power structures, but on inner landscapes. The boundaries are subjective, the maps subject to mood. According to the Equal Employment Opportunity Commission's definition, any conduct may be deemed sexual harassment if it "has the purpose or effect of unreasonably interfering with an individual's work or academic performance or creating an intimidating, hostile or offensive working or academic environment." The hostility or offensiveness of a working environment is naturally hard to measure by objective standards. Such vague categorization opens the issue up to the individual psyche.

The clarity of the definition of sexual harassment as a "hostile work environment" depends on a universal code of conduct, a shared idea of acceptable behavior that we just don't have. Something that makes one person feel uncomfortable may make another person feel great. At Princeton, counselors reportedly tell students, If you feel sexually harassed then chances are you were. At the university's Terrace Club, the refuge of fashionable, left-leaning, black-clad undergraduates, there is a sign supporting this view. It is downstairs, on a post next to the counter where the beer is served, often partially obscured by students talking, cigarettes in hand: "What constitutes sexual harassment or intimidating, hostile or offensive environment is to be defined by the person harassed and his/her own feelings of being threatened or compromised." This relatively common definition of sexual harassment crosses the line between being supportive and obliterating the idea of external reality.

The categories become especially complicated and slippery when sexual harassment enters the realm of the subconscious. The Princeton guide explains that "sexual harassment may result from a conscious or unconscious action, and can be subtle or blatant." Once we move into the area of the subtle and unconscious, we are no longer talking about a professor systematically exploiting power for sex. We are no longer talking about Hey, baby, sleep with me or I'll fail you. To hold people responsible for their subtle, unconscious actions is to legislate thought, an ominous, not to mention difficult, prospect.

The idea of sexual harassment — and clearly when

you are talking about the subtle and unconscious, you are talking about an idea — provides a blank canvas on which students can express all of the insecurities, fears, and confusions about the relative sexual freedom of the college experience. Sexual harassment is everywhere: it crops up in dinner conversations and advertisements on television, all over women's magazines and editorial pages. No one can claim that Anita Hill is an unsung heroine. It makes sense that teenagers get caught up in the Anita Hill fury; they are particularly susceptible to feeling uncomfortable about sexuality, and sexual harassment offers an ideology that explains "uncomfortable" in political terms. The idea of sexual harassment displaces adolescent uneasiness onto the environment, onto professors, onto older men.

The heightened awareness of the potential for sexual encroachment creates an atmosphere of suspicion and distrust between faculty and students. Many professors follow an unwritten rule: never close the door to your office when you and a female student are inside. One professor told a male teaching assistant I know that closing the door to his office with a student inside is an invitation to charges of sexual harassment. If keeping the door open is not enough to ward off the perception or reality of sexual harassment, the authors of *The Lecherous Professor*, an early book of essays about sexual harassment, warn faculty that "if a situation is potentially threatening, a colleague can always be asked to sit in on student-teacher conferences."[6] Although these policies may reduce the likelihood of sexual harassment charges, they also increase the amount of sexual tension between students and professors. The open door or the extra faculty member only draws attention to the potential for a sexual dynamic between professor and student. They promote the idea that professors are more interested in bodies than minds.

The inflamed rhetoric against harassment implies that all women are potential victims and all men are potential harassers. "Men in the Academy," an essay in the book *Ivory Power,* vilifies the male academic so effectively that the author is forced to acknowledge that "nonetheless, not all male professors harass female students."[7] That this need even be said is evidence that this perspective is spiraling out of control.

The irony is that these open doors, and all that they symbolize, threaten to create barriers between faculty and students. In the present hypersensitive environment, caution and better judgment can lead professors to keep female students at a distance. It may be easier not to pursue friendships with female students than to risk charges of sexual harassment and misunderstood intentions. The rhetoric surrounding sexual harassment encourages a return to formal relations between faculty and students.

The university, with its emphasis on intellectual exchange, on the passionate pursuit of knowledge, with its strange hours and unworldly citizens, is theoretically an ideal space for close friendships. The flexible hours combined with the intensity of the academic world would appear to be fertile ground for connections, arguments over coffee. Recently, reading a biography of the poet John Berryman, who was also a professor at Princeton in the forties, I was struck by stories about his students crowding into his house late into the night to talk about poetry. These days, an informal invitation to a professor's house till all hours would be a breach of propriety. As the authors of *The Lecherous Professor* warn, "Contacts outside of class deserve thought. Student-teacher conferences should be held in appropriate settings."[8]

In combating sexual harassment, feminists must necessarily distrust the intimacy of the academic environment. They must necessarily distrust a male professor having lunch with a female student. In *Ivory Power,* this is offered as a male professor's typical attitude: "In a classroom setting it is entirely appropriate that personal and professional lives be separated. However[,] undergraduates doing [honors] research and graduate students [are] becoming junior colleagues; a close personal relationship is to be encouraged."[9] In the eyes of the author, this is an outrageous position, one that precipitates sexual harassment. That this professor's harmless comment is so seditious, that it is used as an illustration of dangerous attitudes among male faculty members, indicates the vehemence of the feminist desire for separation between professors and students.

Feminists concerned with sexual harassment must fight for an immutable hierarchy, for interactions so cleansed of personal interest there can be no possibility of borders crossed. Although this approach to education may reduce the number of harmful connections between teachers and students, it may also reduce the number of meaningful connections. The problem with the chasm solution to faculty-student relations is that for graduate students, and even for undergraduates, connections with professors are intellectually as well as professionally important.

In an early survey of sexual harassment, a law student at Berkeley wrote that in response to fears of sexual harassment charges, "the male law school teachers ignore female students . . . this means that we are afforded [fewer] academic opportunities than male students."[10] Many male professors have confirmed that they feel more uncomfortable with female students than with male students, because of all the attention given to sexual harassment. They may not "ignore" their female students, but they keep them at arm's length. They feel freer to forge friendships with male students.

The overstringent attention given to sexual harassment on campuses breeds suspicion; it creates an environment where imaginations run wild, charges can seem to materialize out of thin air, and both faculty and students worry about a friendly lunch. The repercussions for the academic community, let alone the confused freshman, can be many and serious.

In an excessive effort to purge the university of sexual

corruption, many institutions have violated the rights of the professors involved by neglecting to follow standard procedures. Since sexual harassment is a relatively recent priority, "standard procedures" are themselves new, shrouded, and shaky. Charges of sexual harassment are uncharted territory, and fairness is not necessarily the compass.

In a recent case a tenured professor at a prominent university was dismissed in a unilateral administrative action, without a faculty hearing, legal counsel, or the calling of witnesses in his defense. Some professors have been suspended indefinitely without a sense of when or what would end the suspension. As an official of the American Association of College Professors framed the problem, "There tends to be publicizing of names at too early a stage, and trigger-quick action to suspend without suggestion of immediate harm."[11]

The American Association of College Professors has issued a statement about such overzealous enforcement of sexual harassment policy, explaining that "sexual harassment — which committee A certainly does not condone — is not somehow so different from other kinds of sanctionable misconduct as to permit the institution to render judgement and to penalize without having afforded due process."[12] This statement emphasizes the danger in looking at sexual harassment as an issue somehow more pressing, more serious, more important, than other disciplinary problems. The reason due process is thrown to the wind is that the pressure is so great, and the issue regarded as so delicate and mysterious, that administrations are overcompensating. They feel that if they deal with the issue swiftly, they are being responsive.

In *The Lecherous Professor*, authors Billie Wright Dziech and Linda Weiner explain why feminists are not concerned with due process:

> Let a single 110-pound nineteen-year-old muster the courage to complain about being fondled or threatened by a Shakespeare professor, and Latin professors, geographers, physicists, architects, engineers, and lawyers are likely to rediscover the bonds that unite them. They will as a chorus mouth platitudes about loyalty to the institution, academic freedom and due process. They will suddenly remember the lyrics to the alma mater.[13]

For Dziech and Weiner, academic freedom and due process are simply more platitudes generated by the old-boy network. They dismiss any concern about fairness with their image of the ranks of male professionals united against the slim victim. Sexual harassment has assumed such grand proportions in the minds of these feminists that they are not concerned with the machinations of the disciplinary system, however Kafkaesque. To many feminists, like Dziech and Weiner, who are interested in cleansing the university of harassers, a few casualties of justice along the way seem like a small price to pay.

The university has become so saturated with the idea of sexual harassment that it has begun to affect minute levels of communication. Like "date rape," the phrase "sexual harassment" is frequently used, and it does not apply only to extremes of human behavior. Suddenly everyday experience is filtered through the strict lens of a new sexual politics. Under fierce political scrutiny, behavior that once seemed neutral or natural enough now takes on ominous meanings. You may not even realize that you are a survivor of sexual harassment.

A student tells me that she first experienced sexual harassment when she came to college. She was at a crowded party, leaning against a wall, and a big jock came up to her, placed his hands at either side of her head, and pretended to lean against her, saying, So, baby, when are we going out? All right, he didn't touch me, she says, but he invaded my space. He had no right to do that.

She has carried this first instance of sexual harassment around in her head for six years. It is the beginning of a long list. A serious feminist now, an inhabitant of the official feminist house on campus, she recognizes this experience for what it was. She knows there is no way to punish the anonymous offender or everyone would be behind bars, but she thinks the solution is education. Like many feminists, she argues that discipline is clumsy, bureaucracy lumbering, and there is no hope for perfect justice in the university. She is more concerned with getting the message across, delineating acceptable behaviors to faculty and students alike, than in beheading professors. She subscribes to a sort of zookeeper school of feminism — training the beasts to behave within "acceptable" parameters.

Many foreigners think that concern with sexual harassment is as American as baseball, New England Puritans, and apple pie. Many feminists in other countries look on our preoccupation with sexual harassment as another sign of the self-indulgence and repression in American society. Veronique Neiertz, France's secretary of state for women's rights, has said that in the United States "the slightest wink can be misinterpreted." Her ministry's commonsense advice to women who feel harassed by coworkers is to respond with "a good slap in the face."[14]

Once sexual harassment includes someone glancing down your shirt, the meaning of the phrase has been stretched beyond recognition. The rules about unwanted sexual attention begin to seem more like etiquette than rules. Of course it would be nicer if people didn't brush against other people in a way that makes them uncomfortable. It would also be nicer if bankers didn't bang their briefcases into people on the subway at rush hour. But not nice is a different thing than against the rules, or the law. It is a different thing than oppressing women. Etiquette and politics aren't synonyms.

Susan Teres of SHARE said, at the 1992 Take Back the Night march, that 88 percent of Princeton's female students had experienced some form of sexual harassment on campus. Catharine MacKinnon writes that "only 7.8% of women in the United States are not sexually assaulted or harassed in their lifetimes."[15] No wonder. Once you cast the net so wide as to include everyone's everyday experience, identifying sexual harassment becomes a way of interpreting the sexual texture of daily life, instead of isolating individual events. Sensitivity to sexual harassment becomes a way of seeing the world, rather than a way of targeting specific contemptible behaviors. In an essay attempting to profile the quintessential sexual harasser, two feminists warn in conclusion (and in all seriousness) that "the harasser is similar, perhaps disturbingly so, to the 'average man.' "[16]

As one peruses guidelines on sexual harassment, it's clear where the average man comes in. Like most common definitions, Princeton's definition of sexual harassment includes "leering and ogling, whistling, sexual innuendo, and other suggestive or offensive or derogatory comments, humor and jokes about sex."[17] MacKinnon's statistic includes obscene phone calls. These definitions of sexual harassment sterilize the environment. They propose classrooms that are cleaner than Sesame Street and Mr. Rogers's neighborhood. Like the rhetoric about date rape, this extreme inclusiveness forces women into old roles. What message are we sending if we say We can't work if you tell dirty jokes, it upsets us, it offends us? With this severe a conception of sexual harassment, sex itself gets pushed into a dark, seamy, male domain. If we can't look at his dirty pictures because his dirty pictures upset us, it doesn't mean they vanish. It means he looks at them with a new sense of their power, their underground, forbidden, male-only value.

Instead of learning that men have no right to do these terrible things to us, we should be learning to deal with individuals with strength and confidence. If someone bothers us, we should be able to put him in his place without crying into our pillow or screaming for help or counseling. If someone stares at us, or talks dirty, or charges neutral conversation with sexual innuendo, we should not be pushed to the verge of a nervous breakdown. In an American College Health Association pamphlet, "unwanted sexual comments, jokes or gestures" are characterized as "a form of sexual assault."[18] Feminists drafting sexual harassment guidelines seem to have forgotten childhood's words of wisdom: sticks and stones may break my bones, but names will never harm me.

Someone I knew in college had an admirable flair for putting offenders in their place. Once, when she was playing pinball in Tommy's Lunch, the coffee shop across from Adams House, a teenage boy came up to her and grabbed her breast. She calmly went to the counter and ordered a glass of milk and then walked over and poured it over his head. She would intimidate obscene phone callers with the line "Listen, honey, I was blow job queen of my high school," and they would inevitably hang up. Most of us probably have less creative ways of handling "sexual harassment," but we should at least be able to handle petty

101

instances like ogling, leering, and sexual innuendo on the personal level.

I would even go so far as to say that people have the right to leer at whomever they want to leer at. By offering protection to the woman against the leer, the movement against sexual harassment is curtailing her personal power. This protection implies the need to be protected. It paints her as defenseless against even the most trivial of male attentions. This protection assumes that she never ogles, leers, or makes sexual innuendos herself.

Interpreting leers and leer-type behavior as a violation is a choice. My mother tells me about the time she was walking down the street in the sixties, when skirts were short, with my older sister, who was then three. A construction worker made a comment to my mother, and my three-year-old sister leaned out of her carriage and said, "Hey, mister, leave my mother alone." My mother, never the conventional sort of feminist, told my sister that the construction worker wasn't hurting her, he was giving her a compliment.

Although my mother's reaction may not be everyone's, this is a parable about individual responses. There is a spectrum of reactions to something like a leer. Some may be flattered, others distressed; some won't notice, and still others, according to some feminist literature, will be enraged and incapacitated. In its propaganda the movement against sexual harassment places absolute value on the leer. According to its rules, whatever that construction worker said to my mother was violating, harmful, and demeaning. According to its rules, my three-year-old sister was right. By rallying institutional authority behind its point of view, by distributing these pamphlets that say leering always makes women feel violated, this movement propels women backward to a time when sexual attention was universally thought to offend. They are saying, as Catharine MacKinnon neatly summarizes it, that "all women live in sexual objectification the way fish live in water."[19] But I think it depends on where you learned to swim.

History offers an example of another time when looks could be crimes, but today feminists don't talk much about what happened to black men accused of "reckless eyeballing," that is, directing sexual glances at white women. Black men were lynched for a previous incarnation of "sexual harassment." As late as 1955, a black man was lynched for whistling at a white woman.[20] Beneath the Jim Crow law about reckless eyeballing was the assumption that white women were the property of white men, and a look too hard or too long in their direction was a flouting of white power. Reckless eyeballing was a symbolic violation of white women's virtue. That virtue, that division between white women and black men, was important to the southern hierarchy. While of course lynchings and Jim Crow are not the current danger, it's important to remember that protecting women against the stray male gaze has not always served a social good. We should learn the lessons: looks can't kill, and we are nobody's property.

All of this is not to suggest that abuses of power are
not wrong. They are. Any professor who trades grades for
sex and uses this power as a forceful tool of seduction de-
serves to face charges. The same would be true if he traded
grades for a thousand dollars. I'm not opposed to stamping
out corruption; I only think it's important to look before
you stamp. Rules about harassment should be less vague,
and inclusive. They should sharply target serious offenses
and abuses of power rather than environments that are
"uncomfortable," rather than a stray professor looking
down a shirt. The university's rules should not be based on
the idea of female students who are pure and naive, who
don't harbor sexualities of their own, who don't seduce, or
who can't defend themselves against the nonconditional
sexual interests of male faculty and students.

Although sexual harassment can be a real and serious
problem, like any other abuse of power, there is a difference between handling individual instances and conducting rigorous, large-scale education campaigns and media
blitzes about the problem. Organizations like Princeton's
SHARE and Harvard's RESPONSE advertise their way of
looking at experience to the incoming students. They put
up posters and give out pamphlets, they have workshops
and counselors and peer counselors and hot lines. A serious concern about substantive abuses of power is one
thing, but transforming discussions of sexual harassment
into the latest craze is another. Alarmist propaganda warning about the sexual dangers lurking in the freshman's fu-

ture is not going to help anyone understand anything any better.

David Mamet's play "Oleanna" dramatizes the consequences of sexual harassment propaganda. A young professor rambles — the self-assured, self-involved rambling of status — and a student listens resentfully. At one point she gets upset, and he puts his arm around her, which she interprets as a sexual advance. He tells her he "likes her" when she asks why he is bothering to help her. The play hinges on the way in which she twists his words and actions to fit into her own puzzled ideological context.

Between the first and second acts, she reports the professor to the tenure committee. Feminism transforms the thick, timid student with an aversion to big words into a full-fledged, jargon-toting, rapid-fire radical. She comes into his office armed with accusations of his classist, sexist, elitist behavior. She thinks he belittles her lack of "privilege." She refers to her feminist group as "My group" and declares that she is acting not as an individual but on behalf of her group. As she gets up to leave, he grabs her by the shoulders to force her to hear him out. This gesture later evolves into her charge of attempted rape. She gives him a list of books, including his own, and agrees to recant her charges if he agrees never to teach them again. He refuses.

Mamet's play is not just a story about words twisted, and the strange origins of false charges, about the uneasy power dynamics between teacher and student. It is not just about two people in the same room at the same time experiencing two wildly different versions of the same event. Mamet gets at the deeper issues always there beneath the he-said-she-said debate that cycles endlessly, fruitlessly on. His play is also an allegory. The student represents a certain kind of no-apologies, no-nuances, no-jokes, it's-our-turn-now feminism. The exchange between the well-meaning, if self-obsessed, professor and the student puffed large with her sense of her own victimization becomes a parable about the political confrontations erupting within universities.

In the final scene the young woman rightfully declares the struggle as one over power. She rightfully notes that the professor hates her because she has power over him. After overhearing many phone calls to his wife, she tells him, victory in her voice, not to call his wife "baby." This drives him over the edge. He has lost everything, his job, his new house, and now she is telling him what to call his own wife. The play seems to accelerate; the action moves fast and hard. He hits her, throws her to the ground, calls her "you little cunt." The tension rattling between them for so long, back and forth in terse, edgy words, bursts into physical action.

In the midst of the violent skirmish, Mamet's message rises above the play's more obvious gritty realism. The student's charges are seen as what they are: a self-fulfilling prophecy. The professor has turned into what she always thought he was. The last words of the play are hers, from her position on the ground: "Yes, that's right, that's right."

Feminists, Mamet warns, will conjure up the sexist beast if they push far enough. By seizing power through dogma, by desiring to purge the university of certain books with the "wrong" values, this brand of feminism ensures a fierce response. In pitting women against men, "her" group against "his" group, the student sets up a struggle for power in which there are no winners. She ends up insulted, assaulted, on the ground, the victim she never was, and he ends up the abusive, ugly man he never was.

Mamet is telling us that the so-called male establishment, sensitive as it is, will not sit back and let its books be banned. It will not accept the accusations without a fight. The girl's group necessarily creates, feeds, and — to use her word — empowers its opposition. This is a movement, Mamet warns, that really will change higher education, but not in the way it seeks to. It will force the university's old guard to defend itself, its jobs, and its books against the timid, inarticulate, even dull student who has risen to power on the crest of the multiculturalist wave.

The transformation of the student that Mamet describes has a more prosaic pace in real life. But the pamphlets about sexual harassment do offer sample cases that translate what seem like everyday occurrences into the language of outrage and political indignation. "Maria is one of two women in a precept [Princeton's word for class]. When her preceptor talks to her about a paper he gets closer than she considers necessary. Lately he has been touching her to get her attention, and has brushed against her several times. She feels very tense and this is affecting her work."[21]

Maybe her preceptor is thinking about her sexually and maybe he isn't. Maybe he's nearsighted and that's why he's leaning close to read her papers. Maybe that's just the way he is. In the present environment, this mild set of behaviors constitutes an offense. She can report him. She can seek counseling for this traumatic experience.

Here's another one involving peers: "Marlene and Bill live on the same floor of the dorm. Bill recently approached her and asked her out. She politely declined. Since then, every time Bill sees Marlene he comments on her appearance. Last night Bill walked into her room uninvited. She asked him to leave. He persisted, telling her that she must be hung up about sex, or unliberated, and finally left. Marlene is nervous, depressed, angry. She is afraid to continue living in the dormitory."[22]

Bill is not the picture of maturity, but what's really strange about this exemplum is Marlene's reaction. Maybe from Bill's perspective he likes her. He's nervous around girls and finally got up the courage to ask her to go to a party with him. He told her she looked good in her new suede miniskirt. That didn't help. In his awkwardness, he made a stupid joke about the sexual revolution. He thought it would make her laugh. It didn't — instead she thought it was sexual harassment.

But of course the worry here is not Bill. Bill will be

fine. The worry is these distraught women. What's going to happen to this hypothetical Maria and this hypothetical Marlene when they walk through Central Park, when they go to buy a slice of pizza, when they go to the movies, when they go to parties? The streets are full of perilous compliments. Such sensitive souls (and their sensitive bodies) are not going to get along well in our difficult world. If organizations like SHARE and RESPONSE foster and nurture this kind of perspective, their hothouse flowers are going to wilt in the light of postcollege day.

These somber pamphlets don't have much practical value, but they do send messages, they do promote their perspective. Their authors are interpreting everyday experience. They are giving names to nebulous human interchange. If the name we are given is sexual harassment, then that name will affect that experience and how we think about that experience.

As feminists interested in the issue themselves argue, "Many have difficulty recognizing their experience as victimization. It is helpful to use the words that fit the experience, validating the depths of the survivor's feelings and allowing her to feel her experience was serious."[23] In other words, these feminists recognize that if you don't tell the victim that she's a victim, she may sail through the experience without fully grasping the gravity of her humiliation. She may get through without all that trauma and counseling. Buried within this description of helping students overcome the problem of "recognizing their experience as victimization" is the nagging concern that the problem may pass unnoticed, may dissolve without political scrutiny. To create awareness is sometimes to create a problem.

Education about sexual harassment is not confined to the space of freshman week. As sexual harassment is absorbed into public discussion, it enters grade schools as easily as colleges. An article in *New York* magazine documents the trickle-down effect: "After her first week at a reputable private school in Manhattan, 8-year-old Alexandra didn't want to go back. A 9-year-old boy had been harassing her: 'He said he wanted to hump me.' She wasn't sure what 'hump' meant."[24]

The article describes what happened when Alexandra discovered the name for her traumatic experience. She was listening to Anita Hill's testimony on the radio when she suddenly exclaimed: " 'That's what happened to me! He didn't touch me, but his words upset me!' " The article concludes that "Alexandra's first lesson in sexual harassment may not be her last, but thanks to her parents, who listened to her, believed her and supported her, she'll at least be better prepared to deal with sexual abuse than the women and men of Anita Hill's generation."[25] As Alexandra grows up, will she be better able to deal with sexual abuse, or will she just see it everywhere she looks? Will she blur the line between childish teasing and sexual abuse for the rest of her life? The prospect of a maturing generation of Alexandras, sensitized from childhood to the issue of sexual harassment, is not necessarily desirable from the feminist point of view. As Joan Didion wrote in the sixties, certain segments of the women's movement can breed "women too sensitive for the difficulties of adult life, women unequipped for reality, and grasping at the movement as a rationale for denying that reality."[26]

Responding to sexual harassment in its most expansive definition purges the environment of the difficult, the uncomfortable, and the even mildly distasteful. Feminists concerned with sexual harassment reproduce their own version of Charlotte Perkins Gilman's *Herland*, based on the absence of messy sexual desire. Although it takes some imaginative leaps to get there, their version of Herland is a land without dirty jokes, leers, and other instances of "unwanted sexual attention." Whether or not visions of a universe free from "sexual harassment" are practical, the question becomes whether they're even desirable.

Mary Koss, author of the *Ms.* magazine survey of rape, writes that "experiencing sexual harassment transforms women into victims and changes their lives."[27] Koss sees this transformation into victimhood as something caused by sexual harassment, an external event. In Koss's paradigm, after the student has been harassed, her confidence is perilously shaken, her ability to function and trust men disrupted forever. She sees the "lecherous professor" as the agent of transformation. She does not see that it is her entire conceptual framework — her kind of rhetoric, her kind of interpretation — that transforms perfectly stable women into hysterical, sobbing victims. If there is any transforming to be done, it is to transform everyday experience back into everyday experience.

The Mad Hatter's Tea Party

I am listening to a lecture given by an eminent scholar with a feminist-Marxist-poststructuralist bent. In his cashmere suit, with his soft cashmere voice, he talks about the "hybridization of the postcolonial female discourse." Sitting on a wooden chair, I am trying to focus on his words. His lecture is deliberately opaque: he talks about "the inside of the outsiders' insiderness." As I lose my concentration the words break down into syllables that don't make sense. I hear the rise and fall of the speaker's cadences without the meaning. And then I remember a voice from childhood, "Beware the Jabberwock, my son."

Sometimes I do feel like Alice in Wonderland falling down the rabbit hole, tumbling through the dirt tunnel into another world, "curiouser and curiouser," wondering what on earth the White Rabbit is talking about. In classes and lectures, at Take Back the Night marches, I sometimes lose my bearings, like Alice, and everything seems upside down and backward.

In a conversation about how terrible it is that a professor made a dirty joke in class, I offer my opinion. Someone tells me that I don't understand the humiliation, the violence, of these comments. We look at each other, nothing more to say, our argument backed against a wall.

In a class on American literature a fierce controversy rises up about Edith Wharton. Someone argues that her novels are elitist and bourgeois. Another person adds that Wharton is antifeminist, because some of her female characters are insufficiently developed. Someone claims that Edith Wharton doesn't do justice to May Welland, the shallow blond character in *The Age of Innocence*. I say May Welland is not a flesh-and-blood person with an existence independent of how Edith Wharton thinks of her, she is a character in a book. I begin to argue against looking at literature for well-rounded characters, and one of the men in the class interrupts me with the statement, You are wrong, Edith Wharton's characters are necessarily antifeminist because within the hegemonic male discourse, it is impossible for the female voice to be empowered.

Sitting around the seminar table in my classes, I sometimes feel like I am at the Mad Hatter's tea party. Either I'm crazy or they are. I feel like I am Alice listening to the Mad Hatter tell riddles without answers, my head spinning. This is a game I don't want to learn, this is a tea party without tea, and I have gone through the looking glass.

◈

As an undergraduate, Sarah wore baggy clothes in shades of brown and burnt orange. Looking at her, you couldn't see any curves or angles, just fabric. Her blond hair was short, and she wore an earring in the shape of a woman symbol.

She was generally quiet in classes. But at the beginning of each semester she would raise her hand to ask why there were only two female writers on the syllabus, or why they had left out poetry written by a recently discovered woman in that period. One day after class she complained to me about the boys who dominated discussion with their male mode of argument, their male logic, their male aggression. She couldn't speak. There was no space for her in the clamoring of phallogocentric discussion. Do you notice how few women ever speak in that class? she asked me once on her way out of class. I reminded her that I always talked in class. That's because you have a masculine style of thinking, she said. A friend of hers nodded knowingly. I knew enough not to be flattered.

When the papers brought news of a serial killer in Montreal shooting a group of women, Sarah wore black. This is just an overt manifestation of covert male tendencies, she spent all day whispering to her friends. She wrote graffiti in the bathroom saying "The Montreal serial killer is all men" in bold black letters.

Sarah's small dorm room was always filled with the unpleasant scent of adopted animals, hurt ones, sick ones, ones with terrible skin diseases. One after another, she rescued them from the street, and she would keep them until her roommates forced her to give them away.

Sarah had lots of friends who told her their problems. She was somehow drawn to people who burst into tears all the time, or people who tried to kill themselves at parties. She was drawn to alcoholics and hypochondriacs and people who got themselves into bad relationships. She was attracted to the self-destructive, the brooding, and the out of control. You've got to respect yourself, she'd tell them patiently over cappuccino, you've got to have more self-esteem.

Sometimes, in the middle of a conversation about abortion or wage inequality or the glass ceiling in corporations, Sarah would interject: While we're having this discussion a Latino woman is being mutilated in the Bronx. While we're talking about this several children are being molested by their father. When she disagreed with your argument she would attack your upper-middle-class prejudices, your male prejudices, your elitist, ethnocentric prejudices, and whatever other prejudices she could uncover in your woefully incomplete worldview. If you weren't on your guard and a word like "freshman" or "Indian giver" slipped into your conversation, she would just walk away without a word.

Sarah once told me about her fantasy of creating the ideal university. It would be free from all hierarchy. There would be no grades, and she would accept everyone who wanted to attend. Students would be encouraged to write what they wanted to write and say what they wanted to say. People would read comic books and watch MTV and create their own syllabus around their own interests. No one would be discouraged. No one's work would be compared with anyone else's work. There would be no elitism or sexism. Professors would teach on a rotating system, and they would all be women and members of other oppressed groups. Classes would take place in wide-open spaces; in the spring they would be conducted outside. Once Sarah got started drafting this plan she went on, breathless and flushed, for nearly an hour.

When I asked her about the literature that would be read and written in this university, she said oppressed people would write about being oppressed, women would write about being women, and everyone would read only these books and understand. Wait — I stopped her — you may be abolishing existing hierarchies, but what you're establishing is worse. It's a new aristocracy. What you are talking about is just a new hierarchical system based on birth, where the oppressed, like English kings and queens, would ascend to the throne. But Sarah didn't agree. She told me that I was making a reactionary argument and that I didn't understand anything about turning the tables.

Once, in a real class in our real university, Professor X passed around a book with a photograph of Maud Gonne, and he read aloud the poem William Butler Yeats wrote to her, "No Second Troy." He told the class that when he looked at the picture of Maud Gonne, he could understand why Yeats was so in love with her for so long. Sarah got up and said that she had to leave.

Professor Y told Sarah that he liked her hairstyle, that it looked less severe than when she first got it cut. I was there when he said it, and I watched her expression. Once he left the room, I tried to calm her — he meant well, he was trying to be friendly in his awkward way — but she was outraged. What makes him think he can say that to me? she asked. That is sexual harassment.

In Professor Z's class I once had an argument with another female student who was claiming that Robert Lowell was a misogynist. At one point Professor Z said, Let's continue this discussion, I'm actually enjoying this. Sarah later told me that what happened in class was practically pornographic. She said Professor Z was no better than a gas station attendant watching a pornographic video and getting off on a cat fight.

Sarah wrote a fifty-page paper about how one campus library had a feminine design and one had a masculine design. She wrote about the curves and open spaces of one library and the columns and linear structure of the other.

She stayed up all night every night for a week writing the paper and laboriously drawing the floor plans. She got an A.

Sarah was one of the organizers of Take Back the Night her junior year. In the speak-outs, she told the story of something that happened freshman week. She went to a party, got drunk, and blacked out. The next morning she woke up with no memory but with the knowledge that she had been raped. She was just out of high school, she would never have agreed to sex, so she knows it was rape. After she realized what had happened she took a bath and two showers. At the speak-out Sarah announced that she thinks of it still, in flashes, when she is at a party, after her first sip of beer, when she goes into a dark room. And she thinks of it when Professor Q looks at her legs through a whole lecture.

Sarah mentioned at the speak-out that she traced her sexual abuse to an earlier moment in her history. After many months of therapy, she remembered that an uncle told her dirty stories about the birds and the bees when she was four. She remembered sitting on his knee, feeling violated and knowing something bad, something beyond her years.

Other than that episode with her uncle, Sarah's past was always mysterious. Even her closest friends knew only that she was from New York City and that her parents had an unhappy marriage. People just assumed from the scorn she had for preppies, from the way she held the word so

119

uncomfortably in her mouth, that she was "underprivileged." She wore secondhand clothes with strange patterns that didn't fit. Every now and then she would wake up at six in the morning and go to Dollar-a-Pound in Boston and buy bags of faded clothes in faded fashions for a dollar a pound. She wore her shoes until they had holes, or until someone commented that she was tormenting herself by walking on nails.

One day I ran into her and her parents in a restaurant in New York. After that she told me about her shadowy origins. I learned that what Sarah hadn't talked about all those years was her parents' Fifth Avenue apartment, the house in Southampton, the horseback-riding lessons she loved as a child. She hadn't talked about the check her parents sent her every month.

Sarah wrote her senior thesis about her great-grandmother Elizabeth Mary Phelps, an unknown lady poet from the turn of the century. She discovered her great-grandmother's poetry in the attic of her family's house in Amherst. Sarah told me that Elizabeth Mary was a better poet than T. S. Eliot, Wallace Stevens, and the other white men that have been canonized by generations of white male professors. The title of her thesis was "Captive Bird: The Conflict Between the Artistic Spirit and Domestic Responsibility."

When I last saw Sarah she was on her way to Prague. She told me she was going to spread the feminist word through Eastern Europe.

◈

Not all feminists wear flannel shirts and big sweatshirts; not all of them cut their hair. The most outspoken feminists I have known dieted, exercised, and gossiped about boys.

With her green eyes, her pale skin, and her long red hair, Lauren was striking. She looked like the fantasy heroine of a Harlequin romance. She wore clothes that were tighter and brighter than everyone else's. And lipstick. She always wore some conspicuously purple shade of lipstick. Lauren did women's studies inside and outside the classroom. She would argue about feminism with anyone willing to go a few rounds.

Lauren and I recently got into a long argument about Naomi Wolf. Lauren said that as long as you are in control of your own attempts to be beautiful, no matter what they are, then they are positive and life-affirming. Apparently the idea here is that beauty is a beast that must be captured and controlled. Everything is fine as long as you are holding the leash.

I said that Wolf's divisions were entirely artificial: wrinkle cream is always evil, but lipstick is good, as long as you want to use it, as long as you aren't using it because you feel that you have to. Wolf says she loves fashion magazines in the same breath that she says they have caused the anorexia epidemic. Wolf's argument walks a line so fine, it seems to vanish, I said. But Lauren thinks that Wolf is cele-

121

brating female sexuality while simultaneously pointing out how the backlash against women constructs images of beauty that make women feel bad about themselves. Myself, I've never been able to understand how the "backlash against women," that mysterious force lumbering through our consciousness, can actually "construct" anything. But this was an argument we could never resolve.

Lauren had a circle of friends who were also fashionable feminists. Ada studied political theory. She wanted to be president or maybe just a senator. She walked fast and talked faster. She exuded competence and organization and didn't seem to lounge around as much as the rest of us. Ada ate cornflakes and a banana for breakfast every day and read the newspaper with thin-lipped determination. She wrote well-researched papers on the objectification of women. But at night she would be transformed by giggles, makeup, and long, tight black dresses.

Cordelia wore hoop earrings and sometimes pretended to be dumber than she was. Tall and blond, she wore tight shirts and lots of scarves and took classes in feminist theory. Once she came back from class exhilarated by an exercise they had done. At the beginning of class, they held hands in a circle, and everyone told their matriarchal lineage — their mother's name, their grandmother's name, their great-grandmother's name — as far back as they could. Cordelia read the feminist theory that was imported from France along with her perfume. She talked about female *"jouissance,"* the French feminist Helene

Cixous's word for female bliss, a sort of poststructuralist literary equivalent of orgasm. Cordelia and Lauren
talked about the importance of sisterhood, but when
Cordelia made the discovery that her boyfriend had
cheated on her, she said, What really bothers me is how
totally ugly she is.

These were girls who knew how to put on eyeliner.
These were girls who showed more leg, stomach, and
cleavage than most. Sometimes they went to parties at the
exclusive all-male finals clubs. Sometimes they competed
over boys. They also shouted at Take Back the Night and
organized women's discussion groups. They wrote papers
about patriarchal discourse. They wrote outraged stream-
of-consciousness articles in alternative campus publica-
tions about how terrible and demeaned they felt when men
looked at them in the street, articles filled with run-on sentences running on rage.

At a costume party one year, Cordelia and Lauren appeared as a piece of performance art. They dressed as "the
Male Gaze." They wore identical green dresses, but Cordelia's had pink flowers painted on it and Lauren's had
breasts painted over her breasts. Cordelia carried a sign
saying "How Women See Themselves," and Lauren carried
a sign saying "How Men See Women."

I wondered at the time if Cordelia really saw herself
reflected in an innocent, feminine, floral pattern. No one
ever asked Cordelia, Lauren, and their friends the obvious
question: Do you want men to look at you or not? The

123

answer is clearly both at once, yes and no. The answer is sometimes, maybe, not really, of course. The answer contains the central confusion of their position in the community. In truth, Cordelia and the others would be annoyed if men didn't turn to look at them when they walked into a room.

The obvious split between rhetoric and behavior, between the image voiced and the image projected, left these fashionable feminists open to attack. They were sometimes called hypocrites, especially after some of them dressed as prostitutes for a costume party. But they would answer these accusations with self-assurance. They would claim that fashion is an ideological statement: we dress this way because we want to. We are exhibiting our control over our own sexuality. We are empowering ourselves.

The fashionable feminists swung between extremes: extremes of anger and extremes of dress. They mixed daring with self-righteousness, they mixed flaunting with not wanting to be objectified. They mixed "Keep your eyes to yourself" with "Look at me." In dressing the way they did, they bred daily conflicts for themselves, daily political struggles.

If you wear a tiny skirt and a tight shirt, in this world, such as it is, people are going to stare. If their stares enrage you, you are going to be enraged. As they read more feminist theory than most people and wore less clothing than most people, these girls crafted their bimbo image out of contradiction. Their sexual bravado and their provocative clothing coexisted uneasily with their intellectual and emotional contempt for male gazing.

In the end, what is interesting about these feminists is not their hypocrisy, but their paradox. The conflict inherent in their stance characterizes women in flux, women suspended between concerns of sexual liberation and concerns of sexual harassment. Naturally they loved Naomi Wolf's ideas about the beauty myth, because Wolf's blend of feminism smooths over precisely this contradiction. You can wear lipstick, as long as you like it, even though the cosmetic industry is an instrument of oppression. It's great that men stare at you at a party, but they shouldn't stare if you don't want them to, and they shouldn't stare on the street. Wolf's ability to have it both ways, to write this paradox into her polemic, to make it seem "empowering" instead of schizophrenic, makes her the ideal spokesperson for this kind of feminism.

The truth is that there is a logic to this contradiction. With their will to power, Lauren and her friends are a Nietzschean breed. They take status where they can get it. Socially and intellectually, the university rewards women for being sexy and rewards them for being oppressed. Declaring oneself oppressed translates into definite social currency, and so does sexual attractiveness. Contradictory as these sources of strength may seem, these women draw from both. They are not about to surrender the opportunities and benefits offered to the flirt or the militant feminist.

For these women, ideas of violation and liberation blend into an attitude not so easy to decipher from the outside. Desire, anxiety, feminism, and ambition clash, and what emerges is this strange new hybrid species: the radical cover-girl chic feminist.

❖

Amanda is a graduate student in English. Unlike most of us ragged students of literature, she dresses impeccably, in pearls, gold earrings, matching jackets and skirts, silk shirts tucked in, her blond hair short and neat. She looks as though she ended up in graduate school by taking a wrong turn on her way to a business school interview.

She has no particular passion for literature, but she does have a passion for trends in literary criticism. Feminist literary criticism is a blossoming field; women's-studies shelves in bookstores are expanding; journals of literary criticism are filled with essays on "en-gendering" something or other; and most important to Amanda, feminists do relatively well in the job market. Amanda follows the scent of success. She knows with the certainty of graphs and charts what will look good in job letters and sound good in job interviews.

Her conversation is peppered with words like *inscription, appropriation, hegemonic,* and *transgress.* In her world, things don't just exist, they are "constructed." People don't just write, they "position themselves within the dominant discourse." These words can of course be useful; every field from medicine to architecture has its own vocabulary. But they can also function as easy shortcuts, as passwords to a world of prefabricated thought. They offer a way not to think for yourself. By talking about how a character is "inscripted" into a text, the insecure graduate student evokes the already established. Words like *subversive* can be crutches for the inarticulate. Who needs an imagination of one's own if the path has already been cleared (and cleared and cleared)?

Once, in class, Amanda said, "I feel written out of Blake's poetry as a woman." But feelings have nothing much to do with Amanda's comments. I had three different classes with her, and one week she made the same comment in each class about three different poems by women: they reminded her of "Irigaray's notion of female negativity." Amanda's remarks in class often included the word *other*, as in "They appropriated the discourse of the other."

In another class, we were reading an Emily Dickinson poem about a balloon that is torn in a tree and falls into the ocean. This is obviously a poem about rape, Amanda said. The rest of the class agreed. The professor agreed. I said that I didn't see rape in the poem, and they pointed to the tearing as evidence of violence and violation. Amanda said that Dickinson had "dehumanized the creature." I pointed out that the creature was after all a balloon and it was hard to dehumanize a balloon. But everyone looked at me like I was disrupting the flow of class discussion again, being too literal-minded again.

After a piece I wrote questioning the existence of the date-rape crisis appeared on the *New York Times* op-ed page, several of Amanda's close friends wrote a petition against my views. They accused me of not accepting "the extent to which gender, race and class were radically given voice in the academy." It was a strange accusation, since I hadn't written about race or class at all. They took the petition to professors and got a few to sign. They took it to the graduate students' committee meeting. They posted it in the English department and put copies in all of the mailboxes. One of Amanda's male comrades, also a member of the "gender, race and class" set, told me that I was "cruel" to women. Another told me that he had signed their "communal production" even though he and I were friends, because "politics is more important than friendship." The communally produced letter triumphantly declared that my reference to Henry James, a dead white male author, betrayed my conservative bent. Even though we all had classes together, they had decided that to look at me or speak to me would be to betray the cause.

But Amanda and I still talked. She showed me a paper she wrote called "The Post-Colonial Intellectual: Chuck D." Amanda's papers were full of puns. There was lots of "(dis)membering," "(re)membering," and "(en)gendering" in her work. With this rhetorical style, Amanda shows off her sensitivity to the latest critical trends as surely as a woman of high fashion goes out and buys the latest hat shown in the pages of *Vogue,* however silly, to show off her own fashion sense. Puns and parentheses and dashes are badges of membership in the in-group of subversive leftist literary critics. Her puns are part of an aesthetics of clique — they are winks at the audience, demonstrating that Amanda knows what's ironic and what's serious, what's political and what's profound.

In college Amanda walked out of the movie *Blue Velvet,* because she thought it was violent, voyeuristic, pornographic, and sexist. Later, after hearing everyone talk about how brilliant it was, how daring, how funny, how true, how interesting, she quietly decided that she had been wrong about *Blue Velvet* and joined in singing its praises.

For Amanda there are no distinct lines between classroom and home. All of her thoughts cross the borders. She talks about "triangulation" and "the commodification of desire" with the man who would be her boyfriend if that word wasn't a patriarchal construction of bourgeois society. "Sometimes you treat me in this postcolonial way," she complains to him. She thinks of certain sexual acts between them as "subversive" and "transgressive."

Amanda does not spend hours milling through yellow manuscripts in the library's rare-books room. She does not have a couple of drinks and argue about Milton's *Paradise Lost.* Altogether, Amanda is not the dreamy head-in-the-clouds, nose-behind-the-books sort of graduate student. In fact, she does not waste too much time with the books themselves but instead devotes herself to the books written about the books themselves. She has not read *Clarissa*, for instance — who could plow through more than a thousand pages? — but she has read at least ten books written about *Clarissa*. With her shining analytical mechanisms, her gears turning toward the job market, she reminds me of a well-polished machine. She has mapped out popular theory, churned out the requisite papers, and calculated her way into the profession. If she'd made it to business school she would have become a millionaire by now.

They call themselves the new men or antisexists. The less enlightened call themselves feminists, but most prefer the less presumptuous "profeminists." The new men are not interested in feminism; they are devoted to it. They are not men who sometimes think about gender; they are men who study feminist theory. These are men who are active feminists, who attend seminars and marches and workshops.

These are the J. Alfred Prufrocks of our generation. They have "heard the mermaids singing, each to each," and they strain to listen even though the song is not for them. Like Prufrock, these are men who grapple, who see every side of an issue even if it paralyzes them. Nearly every position they take is shaded by descriptions of how *tough, complicated,* or *difficult* it is. As males, and as people who repudiate traditional conceptions of masculinity, these pro-feminists have a lot of equivocating to do. They couch the inconsistencies that inevitably arise from their position in a rhetoric of sensitivity: their confusion and contradictions become *humility, caution,* and *introspection.*

Peter is not conventionally handsome. He is short, plump, and wears glasses. He looks nervous, years of facing schoolyard bullies still show on his face, but as he talks about feminism his face lights up. His voice steadies. His vulnerable eyes fill with confidence and authority. He gently corrects my political incorrectness. When I say "girl" he says "woman," when I say "freshman week" he says "first-year-student orientation."

Peter was the only male women's-studies major at a northeastern university. Now that he has graduated, he has started a group of men against sexism. Next fall, the group is going to travel to public and private high schools, giving workshops about sexism and violence against women. Peter is now part of another, larger group, New York Anti-Sexist Men's Action Network. This group's statement includes this declaration: "We reject the notion that masculinity has anything to do with being a man of conscience."

As Peter explains how important this group is to him, I think of him sitting around a giant table with the other antisexist men. When he talks, they listen respectfully. Someone gives a tortured account of recurring rape fantasies. Someone else confesses to reading *Penthouse* all through adolescence. Peter tells me that his closest friends in high school were women. He says that he never really went through a hanging-around-and-drinking-beer-with-the-guys phase. I think of him now, enclosed in the accepting circle of nonsexist men, participating in the anxious rituals of antisexist-male bonding.

Peter explains that embracing antisexist-male ideology does shake up a guy's identity. Constantly questioning his behavior, his emotions, and his interactions, constantly trying to weed out what is conditioned as masculine, does unsettle him sometimes. "It's like pulling a rug out from under yourself. It's like all of a sudden you don't know who you are, you don't know what to wear, you don't know how to interact with people. You ask yourself: who the hell are you anyway?"

But in spite of it all, Peter seems to be doing a pretty good job of self-definition. He has a sense of purpose; he is not caught in the usual mad drift of the recently graduated. Unlike those biding their time waiting tables, working in bookstores, temping in offices, he has found his calling. The pressures of a bad economy and a competitive crowd can't stop him from bringing his message to the city schools.

We are sitting at a sidewalk café. A beautiful woman walks by, and I notice that as Peter bends his head to sip his coffee, he glances furtively in her direction. When the subject of sex comes up, Peter is caught in murky waters. He lowers his voice. Women's bodies raise tricky questions for the antisexist male. There are a lot of thin lines and delicate balances in Peter's answers. There are a lot of pauses. He explains that to be an antisexist male, "you have to be aware of the male gaze and the power stuff behind that." Peter looks at me anxiously and fiddles with the sugar packets.

What, then, are the ethics of seeing a pretty woman on the street? Does he gaze at her? If he's aware of the "power stuff," the complex network of sociopolitical relations involved in that stare, is he allowed to stare? His face darkens for a moment. Yes, he does look at women, sometimes. He can't help it, and he feels bad. He worries that they will misunderstand his stares. He worries that they will get the wrong idea. "As far as they're concerned you're just another asshole saying 'Hey, baby, nice ass,' or something. They don't know that you're an antisexist man when you're looking at them."

On the other hand, Peter does believe in sexual attraction. He says, "Frankly, I don't think sexual attraction to a woman is bad. The feminist community expects that because I'm an antisexist man, I'm not going to be sexual. But no. I love being sexual. It's a tough position to be in." And Peter does seem to be in a tough position, juggling sensitivity and sexuality, politics and libido.

But feminism profoundly affects the nature of his sexual experience. Peter takes the idea that no means no very seriously. He believes that the dangerous realm of sexuality cannot be governed by ambiguity. It cannot be left to the whim of unspoken consent. He believes that consent should be verbal and explicit. I wonder how this sensitive sexuality translates into flesh against flesh, into sitting next to a girl on a couch.

Peter explains that "you have to be aware of people's boundaries, and space, mentally and physically. Rather than just leaning over and kissing somebody, I always ask them, 'Do you really want to do this? Can I do this? Would you like me to do this?' because a lot of women have been conditioned not to be able to say no." Peter says that he continues this line of questioning at each stage of sexual activity. So Peter is talking about more than just no means no, he is talking about "Yes, I've really thought this through and I absolutely want to do this" means yes.

I can tell by the pride in his voice that Peter has been around this bend before. He is used to being praised for his generosity and caution. I know he means well, but an image flashes through my mind: a man says to a woman in his room late at night, "Are you sure you want to do this, are you sure you really know what you're doing?" She doesn't appreciate his condescension and bursts out laughing. But Peter tells me that the women involved are always appreciative of his sensitivity.

In Peter's mind, there seems to be another intersection between sex and feminism. He tells me that someone he knew joined a feminist group because he wanted to sleep with a really sexy feminist and he figured politics was the fastest way to her heart. Peter does not say he himself became interested in feminism to pick up women. He does say, "We have to ask to what extent is a commitment to feminism on the part of a man an attempt to get a woman into bed. To deny that's true at all would be preposterous. I think a commitment to antisexism *should* be attractive."

He goes on to tell me that in the jungle of insensitive men, the male feminist is a rare and welcome flower. "It's so rare that men do this stuff that a common reaction is that women are totally bowled over and say 'Oh my God, you're so wonderful.' " As he smiles, I think of a waiflike feminist looking deep into his eyes as they drink herbal tea together and talk about Andrea Dworkin's new novel.

Tall, dark-haired, and Irish, Marc, a graduate student in political science, is always the first person to raise his hand after a lecture. No matter when you catch him, he always looks as if someone is about to take his picture, as if he is about to run for office. Deeply immersed in profeminist reading and activity, Marc has organized groups to talk about men in feminism.

In Marc's image of the ideal world, people exist along a bisexual continuum. He says that as far as he is concerned, Robert Bly's "soft man," with his quiche-loving seventies sensitivity, should be an ideal. He is interested, he says, in "deconstructing" gender roles. I ask him whether he means this deconstruction in theory or in life. His answer, awarded with his confident smile, is "Both, of course."

Although he doesn't like the breast-beating guilt of many male feminists, Marc admits that guilt is the generator of a lot of his interest in feminism. He says he's read about male violence against women and recognizes certain impulses he's had but didn't act on. He says he is part of male violence against women. He doubts if there are any men out there who aren't. Even if it's in their early teens, even if it's just trying a little too hard at the school dance. You find it shocking, he says, you want to believe you didn't do it. I try to imagine what Marc could possibly have done so many years ago at that school dance in Ireland that made him feel so bad.

I would imagine that guilt is inherent in any involvement in a movement in which you are identified with the oppressor. It must be hard to sit through meetings where women talk about how all men secretly want to rape women. Or classes about how phallocentric linear thought is. I imagine it must be hard to be the one man in the women's-studies class devoted to the commodification of the female body.

For men in feminism, there is an assumption of guilt. The original sin is being born a man. Embracing an ideology with "phallocentric" as one of its gravest aspersions must be hard on those who happen to have a phallus attached to their own body. Marc gave me a copy of one of his favorite books on the subject of profeminism, *Refusing* to *Be a Man*, by John Stoltenberg. In the beginning of the book the author imagines a world full of creatures with an infinite variety of genitals who find pleasure in a myriad of ways. There is no single way to celebrate sexuality. With this grand egalitarian fantasy, Stoltenberg goes to great imaginative lengths to do away with the male organ altogether.

Marc spoke at Take Back the Night at great length about how bad it felt to be a man, and how important it was to do more than talk the talk. As he spoke to the crowd, you could almost hear the painful fluttering of creation beneath his speech — a new Adam being created out of Eve's rib.

Catharine MacKinnon, the Antiporn Star

"Imagine you are tied down to a table. Imagine you are having hot wax poured onto your nipples." This is not phone sex. These are not the confessions of a pedophile. This is the way the distinguished law professor Catharine MacKinnon began her first Gauss lecture at Princeton.

The Gauss seminars on criticism are usually esoteric academic lectures delivered by esoteric academic figures to select audiences. But today the room is packed, the extra chairs are filled, and the audience has spilled over into the aisles and stairways and onto the floors. The French professor moderating the series remarks that of all the Gauss seminars this year, this is the best attended. I arrived half an hour early to get a seat.

With MacKinnon's mixture of extremism and eminence, it's no wonder she has drawn a crowd. People are curious about pornography, but that is not the only thing drawing them to her lectures. MacKinnon's radical ideas about relations between the sexes have profoundly influenced feminism. Her influence extends much further than those Women Against Pornography outside Bloomingdale's shouting "Next time you get raped, don't come running to us" after unbelievers, and further than that woman who burned herself in Minnesota outside a bookstore that sold pornographic books. MacKinnon has been writing about sexual harassment since the seventies, long before it had captured public attention. From women's-studies classes to best-selling feminist books, her theories are always a point of reference. Outspoken, uncompromising, MacKinnon is one of those rare figures, at once at the edge of the political spectrum and a powerful influence on the mainstream.

With the stark image of the archetypal woman, bound, gagged, and molested, tied down to a figurative table, MacKinnon begins to argue her extraordinary case: all pornography should be banned; the First Amendment is overrated; women have no voice in this society; no one hears them when they try to tell the truth about what men do to them; the female experience is one of unremitting violence, abuse, and violation.

MacKinnon's working definition of pornography is "graphic sexually explicit subordination of women." With her category she collapses the distinction between soft core and hard core, between *Playboy*'s coy centerfolds and a photograph of a man burning a woman with a cigarette. MacKinnon puts the multibillion-dollar pornography industry somewhere at the root of all evil. She looks at pornography and sees the destructive force out of which all violence springs: "in pornography there it is, all the abuses that women had to struggle so long even to articulate, all the *unspeakable* abuses."[1] MacKinnon talks about the rapes that occur every few minutes, the incest, the demeaning comments men make to their female co-workers, which all seem to circle back to pornography. Pornography becomes the alpha and omega, the beginning and end of violence against women.

Tall, elegant, MacKinnon slips past every stereotype of the radical feminist. She looks like someone's aunt. She looks like the headmistress of a girls' school. But as soon as she starts talking about the violent subjugation of women that permeates every corner of our apparently free society, her voice breaks through her appearance. The dissonance between her benign image and her fierce message lends power to her words. I have read her writing, and I am still thrown off guard by her lectures. Everything about her is an unlikely juxtaposition, from her potent mixture of mysticism and legalistic logic, her passionate intensity and her poise, her dirty words and her cleansing message, her Republican tweed and her determination to overcome the status quo. In yoking opposites together, defying every expectation at every turn, she effectively packages contradiction as truth. She jostles her audience into questioning their fundamental assumptions, and in the chaos of disrupted expectations she places her point — firm, strong, rigid.

In describing the pornography industry's monstrous power, its far-reaching influence on the darker side of human experience, she endows it with more power than most of us going about our lives relatively uninterested in pornography tend to grant it. Most of us don't think of pornographers as the authors of our suffering and inventors of our characters, but in a generous evaluation of the creative power of pornography, MacKinnon writes, "Pornography can invent women because it has the power to make its vision into reality, which then passes, objectively, for truth."[2]

With grand metaphorical flourishes, MacKinnon compares pornography to the Holocaust, to slavery, to lynching, to torture, grasping at whatever words for evil history offers her. In her desire to establish the dire straits, the life-or-death urgency, of her cause, MacKinnon borrows symbols from other, more accepted instances of oppression. Her symbol envy leads her to bizarre hyperbole: she compared William Kennedy Smith's alleged date rape to lynching in an op-ed piece in the *New York Times*. In her lecture she says at one point, "Even Hitler didn't know how to make killing into sex the way the pornography industry does." Members of the audience shift in their seat. Her reference startles and provokes. I try to unravel what she actually means, how Hitler actually adds to the logic of her argument, but he doesn't clarify or develop her point — instead he raises the emotional stakes.

Catharine MacKinnon, with her model of a pornographic society in mind, believes that pornography should not be protected under the rubric of freedom of speech; to her, pornography is not speech but an act. She argues that pornography is not an idea but a reality, not representation but fact. She argues that pornography doesn't *show* discrimination against women, it *is* discrimination against women and should be banned as such.

Altogether, MacKinnon does not seem interested in freedom of speech. She does not try to cater to liberal esteem for the First Amendment. She does not try to soften the blow against its commonly accepted transcendent value. As MacKinnon utters the words "freedom of speech," her voice fills with sarcasm, boredom, contempt. She seems tired of people evoking this bothersome constitutional detail as if it were an all-powerful protective charm. She thinks that Americans are too busy guarding their freedom of speech to recognize its failure to translate into real social equality. Whose freedom of speech is it, anyway? she asks. From MacKinnon's point of view, free speech is a male privilege, and women have nothing to lose.

One of MacKinnon's most potent, often-repeated arguments for banning pornography is that pornography actually causes violence against women. She does not draw a sketchy connection but instead declares a direct, scientifically charted causal link. As far as MacKinnon is concerned, violence against women crosses the line between the glossy make-believe world of photographs, videos, actors, cameras, lights, and makeup into the real world of flesh, blood, rape, and sex. In order to prove this vital and tricky point, she summons examples of pornography entering into sexual assaults.

She cites a rape in which men explicitly referred to the pornographic video game Custer's Last Stand. She also offers the example of the early pornographic classic *Deep Throat*. After watching men "deep throat" porn star turned antiporn activist Linda Lovelace, men have gone out and nearly choked women during oral sex, MacKinnon claims. Others have attempted to force their wife to perform acts physically impossible, because they saw them in *Deep Throat*.

MacKinnon is trying to make the point that pornography inspires male rapists and perverts. Her vision of culture is this: the ugly acts shown in pornographic pictures come alive and reproduce themselves throughout the culture. Her point is something like Oscar Wilde's: life imitates art.

When MacKinnon pauses for questions, I raise my hand and ask what she would do with a book like *Lolita*. I ask her what she would do if old men were inspired to kidnap, drug, and molest real-life nymphets as a result of the book. I know defending the province of high art is not her highest priority — she believes the importance of expressing oneself pales in comparison to people getting hurt — and I ask if she proposes to ban this book along with other forms of pornography.

She turns her fierce gaze toward me and says, slowly, deliberately, that *Lolita* is a book about the tragedy of child abuse. As she says this, I think of Nabokov squirming in his grave. Nabokov, who wrote "Lolita, light of my life, fire of my loins," was hardly writing an impassioned diatribe against child abuse. He himself said, "I am neither a reader nor a writer of didactic fiction, and . . . *Lolita* has no moral in tow. For me a work of fiction exists only insofar as it affords me what I shall bluntly call aesthetic bliss."[3] But "aesthetic bliss" has no place in MacKinnon's universe. She goes on to explain that if anyone actually followed Humbert Humbert's footsteps, if he took the plot of *Lolita* and literally performed the acts it describes, then he would be "misreading" the book.

I wonder why it wouldn't be misreading for a man to see *Deep Throat* and then go out and choke a woman to death with his penis, or to rape a woman because of a pornographic video game, or hang a woman because of a spread in *Hustler*. It seems to me that there is an assumption in this society that amid the barrage of cultural pressures, citizens internalize right and wrong, that they aren't as impressionable as clay. One presumes that people see *Superman* and don't try to fly, that they see cartoons and don't try to flatten their enemies under trains, that there is some mediation of civilization and the conscious mind between what you see and what you do — but this is not MacKinnon's model of human, or at least male, behavior.

In making her case about male and female responses, MacKinnon bolsters her argument with studies and statistics. She combines her heightened emotional appeal, her nearly mystical accounts of human behavior, with the language of empiricism. MacKinnon crowds complex political beliefs into pseudoscientific formulas. In one such maneuver, she talks about rating men on the "rape myth acceptance scale," as if it were the same casual gesture, the same flick of the wrist, as taking someone's temperature. The rape myth acceptance scale supposedly measures the subject's acceptance of cultural rape myths like "Women like to be raped." By using terms that appear to measure abstractions and vague, subjective quantities with precision, MacKinnon gives her description of male behavior a patina of scientific accuracy.

With the rape myth acceptance scale as her unshakable source of authority, MacKinnon claims that pornography has the power to transform men into beasts. She tells the audience in no uncertain terms that there is definitive proof that watching pornography raises men's rape myth acceptance scale. She assures the audience that when the men we think of as normal men, nice men, watch pornography, they begin to believe that women like to be raped.

Pornography conditions them toward violence. MacKinnon stresses that no men are immune to this tendency.

She suggests that judges and politicians, the men trying to protect pornography, love it themselves, that they keep it tucked under their bed at night, that as consumers they themselves are part of the pornography industry. She argues that justice, far from being blind, sneaks looks at dirty pictures just like males in our culture. In discussing the failure of her proposed antipornography ordinance, MacKinnon argues that judges are just as tainted as other men by base desires. As an example of the perversions of the judiciary system, she mentions a judge who said he would hate to see Yeats's "Leda and the Swan," a poem about Zeus's rape of Leda, banned as pornographic. MacKinnon uses this judge's fondness for this classic poem to point to his predilection, his possible sexual deviance, as if to say "You know what turns him on."

I scan the faces of the men in the audience. Some of them are sympathetic to feminism, and some are even sympathetic to banning pornography. But I wonder if they are insulted by the monkey-see-monkey-do model of male behavior, with its implied vision of the male as monkey. Later even some of MacKinnon's male supporters confess that as much as they admire MacKinnon, they were put off by the portrait of the male that emerged from her lecture.

The role MacKinnon assigns to women is as rigid as the role she assigns to men. As far as she is concerned, women don't like pornography, and if they do it is because

146

they are scared or brainwashed. This idea of MacKinnon's is not so radical. It is one area in which she closes ranks with traditionalists. In our culture, women are not supposed to like pornography.

Lots of women are in fact curious, interested, or even aroused by pornography. But this is not acceptable, either to many feminists or to society at large. If a woman enjoys pornography, then she is considered some kind of masochist or, worse, a traitor. In *Harper's*, one woman devoted a long article to her personal odyssey of renting pornographic videos. The idea that a woman might like pornography, might actually seek it out rather than glimpse it out of the corner of her eye, is so shocking that it warrants an entire tortured article. And it was interesting, it was worth a whole article, because pornography is still forbidden to women, it is still taboo.

MacKinnon says that any woman who thinks she doesn't mind pornography and isn't assaulted daily with male violence in one form or another is deluding herself. MacKinnon thinks that the glaring truth of such a woman's victimization is so painful that she must be desperately trying not to believe it. Then, of course, chances are she's also repressing the terrible things that have happened to her. MacKinnon grants that there is some slim chance — and the sarcasm in her voice tells you it's slimmer than a camel passing through a needle's eye — that she may be one of the handful of lucky ones emerging from patriarchal oppression miraculously unscathed. I have heard this before. It is an accusation that always angers me, because it allows no response. MacKinnon's is the sophisticated political version of the classic grandparent's whine: you don't know what's good for you.

MacKinnon talks about women drugged and beaten into submission, forced as slave labor into the sex industry. She compares the women employed in the sex industry with children:

> Some of the same reasons children are granted some specific legal avenues for redress — relative lack of power, inability to command respect for their consent and self-determination, in some cases less physical strength, or lower legitimacy in using it, specific problems in credibility, problems and lack of access to resources or meaningful self-expression — also hold true for the social position of women compared to men.[4]

So the idea of women as children enters MacKinnon's writing. If you're going to claim that women have as little power and autonomy as MacKinnon claims, then they may as well be children. There is something strange about her equating women in society with children: she herself is as strong a woman as I can imagine. She is not childlike, and she clearly doesn't think of herself as a child. The infantilized position is one she reserves for other women.

With her image of woman as child, MacKinnon echoes the ideas of the Women's Christian Temperance Union in the nineteenth century. Like MacKinnon, the nineteenth-century protofeminists worried about something they called social purity. Instead of pornography, for them prostitution was the metonymy of evil. They spoke of female prostitutes in terms similar to those in which MacKinnon speaks of the women employed in the pornography industry — as if they had no will, as if they had been captured and exploited and forced like slaves to serve the base desires of men. As many historians have noted, this was simply not an accurate portrait of all nineteenth-century prostitutes, and it is not an accurate portrait of all twentieth-century workers in the sex industry. As MacKinnon talks, the ideal of social purity burning in her inflamed rhetoric, you can hear the legacy of the nineteenth century in her voice.

Her political argument is a closed system. There is no way to crack it, no internal contradiction threatening to explode. That's because MacKinnon's is not a political argument, it is a belief system. It is closer to religion than law, and there is no way to sway the true believer. At the height of her emotional pitch, the room fills with palpable tension. The audience is intimidated, enraptured, captivated, motionless. Even the skeptics like me are silent and listening.

As MacKinnon talks about her antipornography ordinance, her eyes burn, her face flushes, her hair begins to fall from her bun. She is fire and brimstone. She is a Puritan preacher with a strong jaw, and her words carry all the positive and negative associations attached to the Puritans — discipline, dogma, sharp lines, New England autumns, and a furious gray path to grace. She surpasses the level of intensity beyond which there is no doubt God is on your side.

The politics professor who introduces her says that reading Catharine MacKinnon was the closest she'd ever come to a religious experience. From MacKinnon's cool glance, I get the feeling thousands of people have said that to her. She must be used to people swooning at her feet, asking her to heal small children. Many people emerge from her lectures using religious language — "She's a prophet" — and it's no wonder.

MacKinnon says that the men who took her class on pornography were "destroyed" by it and had to "reconstitute" themselves. With this telling formulation, she reveals the godlike aspect of her self-image — her project involves the destruction and re-creation of consciousness. She gives her audience a sample of her destructive powers: when a man who identifies himself as a criminal lawyer challenges her with a difficult question, she deflects him with the line Well, that's why I'm up here and you are a criminal lawyer.

No Pollyanna, MacKinnon is all edges, angles, bristles, and tough words. She sprinkles words like "cunt" and "fuck" through her lectures. She repeats the phrase "penis slamming into the vagina" more than once. Even her political metaphors are sexual: "Sexual harassment penetrates us" and it "moves inside of you and becomes you." Sexual imagery, blunt words, this is how she gets her point across.

All of the "fucking" that goes on in her lectures asserts mastery. It asserts her anger, controlled, powerful, focused, instead of fear. She does not avert her glance from the dirty truth. She is not polite. She assures the audience that she's seen more pornography than any of us. Her crude words show that she is not afraid of sex; she just despises it. She does not shrink from pornography; she wants to battle it. She wants to confront and explode pornography head-on, eyes open. Her persona, and her argument, are hard and tough. They will not crack easily under the frequent accusations of prudery.

Presumably MacKinnon is trying to illustrate exactly how pornography injures women, and presumably to do so she cannot avoid the pornographic idiom. But the other justification for the *cunt*s and *fuck*s in her language is that she knows, better than anyone else, that sex and violence sell, and so she uses them to sell her message. MacKinnon does not deliver dry legal briefs that pass for lectures. She knows how to captivate an audience. She packages her message in shock value, in naughtiness, in titillation. With her dirty words and metaphors, she catches people's attention and holds it. It seems as if MacKinnon uses graphic language in her diatribe against pornography to steal its fire. She will be heard by any means necessary.

And the surprising thing is that her words, radical fighting words, travel high and far. People listen, people are convinced. Mary looks like she has just stepped out of the pages of a J. Crew catalog. She is from a small town and a small college in the Midwest. She is the girl next door if there ever was one. But she walks out of MacKinnon's lecture with her beliefs shaken. Her ancestors were Pilgrims and signers of the Declaration of Independence. She memorized the Bill of Rights when she was in fifth grade, and every Sunday she goes to church. But she breaks out of her white-picket-fenced background in thinking that MacKinnon is brilliant, that she is right about women's experience in society. As she listened to MacKinnon's lectures, she realized that the First Amendment, so proudly heralded in her home, is not as simple as she'd always thought it was.

In spite of the success of MacKinnon's lecture, and others like them, pornography is not the most pressing feminist issue on most campuses. True seaminess, in the Forty-second Street, XXX-rated form that MacKinnon emphasizes, doesn't brush against the life of the average college student. Maybe the average college student's boyfriend has a copy of *Hustler* magazine, maybe they once rented a pornographic video to see what it was like, but the pornography industry that MacKinnon describes — with all of its diabolical machinations, the nude dancer under bright lights — takes place far from our world.

But that doesn't mean students don't take stands on pornography. There is often an outcry when pornographic movies are shown on college campuses. Protests have cropped up on all kinds of campuses, from Indiana State University to Wesleyan.

At one slide show about pornography at Harvard, feminist Gail Dines warned an audience of around three hundred mostly female students that the pornography industry has "aggressively targeted college men."[5] At Harvard, when they screened a film about the evils of pornography, people emerged from the room with tears in their eyes. Some say that they had nightmares for a long time afterward.

Although pornography has been getting a lot of media play in the last few years, this is not a brand-new discussion. It's been going on for so long that familiar lines have been carved in the face of the debate. Catharine MacKinnon has been attacked by many feminists, but outspoken, established, and eloquent, she remains steadfast, a cultural commentator. (In spite of her insistence on her own marginal status and voicelessness, she has argued before the Supreme Court.) In response, many feminists have pointed out the danger of curtailing the First Amendment. Many feminists have pointed out that the tools of censorship have been used historically against the most oppressed groups. Many feminists value freedom of speech more than they fear pornography.

But the dangers of MacKinnon's argument travel beyond the threat of censorship. While it's important to guard against potential encroachments on freedom of speech, censorship is by no means the only thing at stake. MacKinnon's Indianapolis ordinance was declared unconstitutional. The truth is that she has not managed to obtain much actual legal space in which to implement her proposed legislation. And although MacKinnon presses on with her practice as well as with her theory, it is her theory that is most dangerous.

The threat is that MacKinnon's radical premises are absorbed into our culture: her pure, crystalline politics is distilled into other, less strident forms. In progressive steps, MacKinnon's *Feminism Unmodified* is modified. Many more mainstream feminists and intellectuals, like Naomi Wolf and Susan Faludi, among others, pick up threads from her work. Many of her early ideas about sexual harassment and pornography are amplified in common feminist positions. It is easy to trace the path from her thoughts to the cocktail-party conversation of an average left-leaning college sophomore.

So MacKinnon reaches her audience. She reaches further than her audience. She has made a radical stance palatable. She is Andrea Dworkin's presentable other half. They often make the same points, with the same examples, and even use the same ardent, sarcastic, tough writing style, but MacKinnon has achieved popular acceptance, whereas Dworkin has not. The *New York Times Magazine* did a recent cover story on MacKinnon entitled "Defining Law on the Feminist Frontier." As the title reveals, the writer was seduced by MacKinnon's contradictions, her poise, her wit. MacKinnon came out of the vanilla prose sounding as normal as baseball and apple pie. Somehow she is not out in left field anymore. MacKinnon's argument finds the public waiting, receptive. In this taut political atmosphere, issues like sexual harassment, rape, and incest are right below the surface of any conversation about women's issues, ready to spring up at any time. MacKinnon has a consistent, sophisticated, passionate ideology ready and waiting.

It's interesting that Camille Paglia, with her dramatic views and her courageous articulation of the unpopular, is always portrayed as crazy, hysterical, while MacKinnon is not. In some sense, they are opposites. Both believe that violence is a natural part of sex, although Paglia thinks that it's good and MacKinnon thinks it's bad. They meet in the extreme, unconventional territory, but somehow MacKinnon comes off in the standard media representation as the brilliant thinker and Paglia comes off as off-the-wall.

MacKinnon has a following. She has enthusiasts who crowd into her lectures and classes. From law schools to women's-studies departments to political science departments, MacKinnon's work is standard fare. Eminent professors place her at the cutting edge of legal and political thought. She also has groupies. As the *New York Times* reported, "Law students would imitate her dramatic voice or dress or even her hair, and line up outside her office, as one put it, 'to have some of that ferocity channeled at them.' "6

MacKinnon's movement is not confined to ivory towers. It has its own grass roots. A friend of mine was walking through Harvard Square and got swept up in a feminist protest outside a newsstand. After realizing that the group was protesting the *Sports Illustrated* swimsuit issue, he started arguing with one of the feminists, saying that he felt the swimsuit issue was really harmless. She got so angry that she spit on him. He walked into the newsstand, listening to chants of "Cut it out or cut it off."

MacKinnon is the explicit example of the implicit trend. The latent conservative strains of other forms of feminism are manifest in her work. MacKinnon is the human bridge between the far right and the far left. People like Senator Jesse Helms support her antipornography movement. She is the embodiment of an unholy alliance between the right wing and feminists. She is willing to join hands with Jesse Helms and anyone else who will recognize the grave threat to society posed by the multibillion-dollar pornography industry.

Someone in the audience confronts her on the issue of her cooperation with the right wing. She says if someone is willing to stand on your side, you don't throw them out. The circle between the far right and the far left closes around her argument. Her single issue burns so brightly that she doesn't seem to care if sex education gets burned in the process, or art, or photographs, or novels, for that matter.

A few weeks after MacKinnon's lecture, I was walking

around Forty-second Street, and the word that came to mind was "dingy" rather than "ominous." Somehow with her image of men turned on and turned into beasts, Mac-Kinnon misses the squalor, the pathos. Her lurid description of pornography overlooks how depressing it can be. How many of these men are compensating for how short they are or how little money they make? She overlooks the numbness, the mechanical way in which they reach into their pockets for money. The joy and elation, the naked will to power, and the male pleasure in subjugating women she describes don't seem to be the whole story.

In her own way, with her melodramatic comparisons to Hitler, MacKinnon is glamorizing the pornography industry and giving it too much credit. She is forgetting that men don't march in the street waving their copies of *Hustler* like flags, knocking over any women in their way. Extreme violent pornography is the seedy underside, the sickness of our culture, not its primary expression of sexual relations, as MacKinnon would have us think.

MacKinnon believes that pornography is not a symptom but a cause. She doesn't believe in Freudian laws of repression, but she should believe in physics — the law of conservation of energy. Banning pornography wouldn't banish base desires, or the will to power, or the will to tie someone to a bedpost and whip them. Driving pornography further underground would not necessarily help the women who work in the sex industry. It would not necessarily lessen the thrill or influence of pornographic images.

What MacKinnon has to offer is not analysis but aphorisms. Her lecture and her writing are filled with lines like "Man fucks woman. Subject verb object." Open, shut. Her one-track approximation of humor can block all trains of thought, all subtlety. Even though MacKinnon is too sophisticated to talk about biological destiny, her open-and-shut one-liners shut men and women into absolute roles.

MacKinnon claims that when she talks about men and women and their roles, she is talking about something culturally conditioned. But with her bluntness, her structural and syntactical assumption of hierarchy, with her "Subject verb object," she may as well be talking about biology. In MacKinnon's vision of the world, women are so downtrodden, men so aggressive, pornography so evil, that good and bad, male and female, are pitted against each other in mortal struggle. In her worldview, it seems, men and women are inexorably locked into their roles. Any woman who claims not to be oppressed, who claims to have overcome her oppression, is deluding herself as far as MacKinnon is concerned. By portraying women as such victims and men as such aggressors, she threatens to solidify these categories with her proposed legislation.

Pornography is about obsession, as Susan Sontag writes; it is a tireless, plotless genre. There is no doubt that MacKinnon has what Sontag labels "the pornographic imagination." It is not coincidence that MacKinnon's lecture and writing follow the linguistic, structural, and formal conventions of pornography. It is not surprising that MacKinnon began her lecture with that image of a timeless woman having hot wax poured on her nipples. Sontag writes that

> the prominent characteristics of all products of the pornographic imagination are their energy and their absolutism ... there are no gratuitous and non-functioning feelings; no musings, speculative or imagistic, which are irrelevant to the business at hand. Thus, the pornographic imagination inhabits a universe that is, however repetitive the incidents occurring within it, incomparably economical.[7]

MacKinnon's pornographic imagination fixates as she writes and rewrites one theme. She is trying to arouse her crowd into activism, into overturning accepted beliefs. Everything is used in the service of her one goal, destroying pornography. As Sontag explains, "The universe proposed by the pornographic imagination is a total universe. It has the power to ingest and metamorphose and translate all concerns that are fed into it, reducing everything into the one negotiable currency of the erotic imperative."[8]

When the antipornographic imagination meets feminism, what comes out is a moral universe, although MacKinnon denies it. What comes out is a universe of victims and aggressors, of violation, subjugation, dominance, and oppression. MacKinnon's brand of feminism is *Star Wars* feminism — there is black and white, lots of moralism, lasers, and dramatic music, but all ambiguity is lost. Free will and flexibility are lost. MacKinnon's well-articulated universe is divided into bold stripes of good and evil. The force is with her, but the force of what? The force is the conservative social atmosphere, and conservative political figures. The force is religious censors, and the force is social fear. In the midst of a confusing, conservative time, she is offering a straightforward conservative message. There are no uncertain terms. Her words exist in a place beyond the shadow of doubt. What she has to offer is pure vision.

Still Looking for
Mr. Goodbar

In the question-and-answer section of Catharine Mac-
Kinnon's lecture, an undergraduate had two questions.
One was about whether it was all right for a feminist organization on campus to show an old pornographic film as
part of an educational program, or whether people might
take voyeuristic pleasure in the film. The other question was
about the computer-animated pornography that students
sometimes stored in the university's computer banks. When
you turned on your computer, an obscene picture appeared
on the screen as the word-processing program started. It's
upsetting, the undergraduate explained. The moderator sig-
naled her to speed up her story — there were so many
hands up in the room and so little time. But MacKinnon
stopped him. This was an important issue. She told the
student that these pictures were violating her right to equal
access to education. The university has an obligation to do
something about them, MacKinnon said, and after the lecture she would tell her what specific steps to take.

Later, after the reception, I watched the undergraduate with the questions walk off through the green and gray of the campus. She was probably still thinking about those pornographic images on the computer, those voluptuous women, cartoon-pink flesh filling her screen in the computer center. I was still thinking about her as she disappeared in the distance. Where was she going, and what did her room look like, pale blue bedspread sprinkled with stuffed animals or bare futon on the floor? Did she sleep with the light on?

Cheltzie, a seven-year-old in Eden Prairie, Minnesota, set state and even federal investigations in motion with her charges of sexual harassment against some boys on her bus who used "naughty language." Like Christopher Columbus and multiplication, sexual harassment was part of her school curriculum. It was something she learned, like the alphabet, about the way things are.

Behind the legal term "sexual harassment" are images of men as hunters and women as hunted. To the seven-year-old, sexual harassment tells a story of princes not so charming and virtuous princesses locked in towers. The dragons to slay are male, and they are after female bodies.

For Cheltzie and others like her, sexual harassment is an issue even in the so-called latency period. The idea of boys as a sexual threat, girls as vulnerable, now takes root early and stubbornly. These are not the facts of life they are learning, but a way of interpreting them.

The naughty words Cheltzie heard on that yellow school bus are no different from the naughty words shouted and muttered in countless school buses over the years. They have no special power to harm, humiliate, or invade. It is the political context that twists them and gives them resonance. Insults have always been part of the push and pull of childhood banter — "Your mother's a —," "So's yours." These are assertions of self, highly charged, full of energy, soaring like Frisbees over the sandbox. But adult preoccupations are crowding the playground. "He said *what* to you?" has broken into the game. The idea of sexual harassment, received at an early age, offers the seven-year-old a powerful talisman against the rough-and-tumble of everyday. Being a victim of sexual harassment is a way to get attention, a way to get the final word. In teaching children to "recognize" sexual harassment, we are training them in victimhood.

It's hard to imagine how Cheltzie, and the other heirs to our cultural obsession with sexual violation, will turn out. We don't have the emotional equivalent of those police pictures for lost children, projected images of what they might look like years later. What happens as they move from seven to eleven to fourteen to twenty-four? What happens as the constant need to be on guard against potential violation moves out of the school bus and into the office? Where does the moral of strength through victimhood lead aspiring judges, artists, and executives? What happens when one begins to identify oneself as the pounded upon, the leered at, the silenced?

163

I started to picture millions of students ripening in this climate, harvested, picked, rotten ones falling to the ground. The rest, in buckets, pickup trucks, what happens to us? How are bodies and minds, how are senses of selves, affected by Catharine MacKinnon, by the fury over Anita Hill, by AIDS, by the fragility all of it implies? It is a question that is too abstract, a column of numbers down a sheet of paper, impossible to calculate. But I can remember myself poised, at the end of college, I can remember what I was thinking.

I had finished packing my books into cardboard boxes at four in the morning. It had been one of those nights, too many cups of coffee and too much time to think about what would happen after graduation. No more hours in the dining hall, gossiping, arguing, no more Saturday nights wandering around Adams House, party to party, no more science classes to skip. It was hard to imagine. I leaned out of my window and looked at the clock tower against the violet sky. I had been looking at that clock tower for years, in different states of mind, elated, depressed, angry, calm, from different angles, from the roof, from parties, and finally I was graduating.

There were only a few hours left to sort things through before the milling crowds of parents and grandparents, robes and cameras, would filter into Harvard Square. The summer stretched ahead full of clean slates, breakfasts alone, and hard-to-picture places where I wouldn't know everything about everyone. Now, of course, all of this doesn't seem as momentous as it did then. It doesn't seem as much like taking your diploma and walking off a cliff. But that morning everything seemed sharper, brighter; everything hit harder, closer, late-adolescent melodrama blending seamlessly with reasonable fears.

I was going through my drawers trying to figure out what to pack and what to throw away. Paper on *Paradise Lost*, pack. Notes on the American Revolution, throw away. Unopened box of condoms, pack. Someone I knew had just tested positive for AIDS. I had been trying not to think about it much, and when I did it was usually from a distance, as something clinical — blood cells, charts, newspapers — something unconnected to me. I could see myself waiting, the sharp, clean hospital smells, patients shuffling by in pajamas, for a doctor in a lab coat and clipboard: come into my office and we'll discuss the lab results. It seemed likely that I might choose the wrong person sometime in the next few months. Not to mention the past.

Then again, I was worried about everything that morning. When I was a baby I was afraid of the wind. I have a memory, although I'm not sure if it's an actual memory or the kind pieced together from parental reminiscence, of sitting in my carriage, feeling the wind against my face, the plaid fabric flapping madly, and crying. It was that feeling I had that morning before I graduated, it was that same intense and general fear.

My usual attitude was that sex might be dangerous,

but then so was driving a car. Risk, danger, and violence were all part of the elaborate car chase of current sexual relations. Who would be hurt was always an open question. At least that's the way I usually felt then. I knew it wasn't just me who thought about sex in terms of risks taken. Look at the movies: Hollywood was, and still is, spinning out movie after movie with the message that killing is sexy and sex kills. Morality mixes with the fear of sex to produce a new kind of erotic thriller: sex and violence are so bound together in our culture that even the bloody mouths of *Bram Stoker's Dracula* can be erotic. Here was the mechanism at work: with sex and violence so integral to our experience, danger begins to turn us on.

But then, of course, the thrill of danger wasn't confined to dark rooms, plush velvet chairs, and film projected against a big screen. That spring had been chaotic. Carpe diem, the poets used to write, and it seemed like I'd been seizing day after day, recklessly, without thinking, for a long time.

When one of my older sisters had come to Cambridge a few weekends before, we had gone to visit a friend of hers. My sister asked him to read my tarot cards, just for fun, and he began to lay the cards down in piles. Ask a question, he said, and my sister asked the fates if I would ever settle down. He turned over the cards, beautifully painted medieval cards, one after another, knights and suns, and the answer was no, not for a long time. The cards predicted a long period of wildness, of restlessness. My sister's friend looked at her helplessly as if to say, What could I do, it was in the cards. It's just a parlor game, he said apologetically as he showed us out.

I poured another cup of coffee and balanced it on the windowsill. The truth was that it wasn't just the appeal of danger I was worried about, the undeniable pull of self-destruction, it was whether my personal life was ever going to make sense. The path seemed to be getting straighter and narrower and the alternatives more threatening than they had been in the past. Ten years from now, all of my friends would be in couples, filing two by two into the Noah's ark of adulthood, leaving me behind, looking up anxiously into the sky. That's what I thought.

At my age my mother was about to get married, and everyone she knew had pins and rings, catching the light, promising happily ever after and settling down. Not that it really worked out that way. Not that I'd have traded places for the world. But early marriage gave my mother's generation security, however illusory, however insubstantial; it gave them something to leap into and hold on to, and that was something I didn't have.

"Knows desire without an object of desire / All mind and violence and nothing felt. / He knows he had nothing more to think about / Like the wind that lashes everything at once." Those were the last lines of a Wallace Stevens poem I had studied earlier that year, and that was how I felt that morning: like the wind that lashes everything at once.

I am spiraling out of control, I thought to myself, images of the past spring running through my head, spiraling
out of control. I had been thinking about everything, including sexuality, in terms of control. So did most people
around me. Whether it was getting it, keeping it, needing it,
wanting it, sex always seemed to come back to control. Control was not just a vocabulary. It was at the heart of our
actions, the way we felt and thought about sex. Most people
I knew, myself included, measured their behavior with some
internal barometer of control, the dial wavering between
extremes of release and extremes of self-restraint. I knew it
hadn't always been like that. In the sixties and seventies, sex
was about expression and orgasm, at least in theory; it was
the streamlined optimism of Erica Jong's "zipless fuck," it
was middle-aged couples in John Updike novels swinging
from bed to bed, heralding free love and open marriage. But
these days even the wildest, most carefree of hedonists I
knew framed their adventures in terms of control lost.

In the title story of Susan Minot's *Lust*, the heroine
floats from bed to bed and winds up feeling diminished.
Minot's always-sensitive female characters lie back and let
experience wash over them. They abdicate responsibility,
they give the impression of being swept up, carried along,
feet off the ground, which is to say that they are not in
control. The strange thing is that the ultrafeminine passive
stance of Minot's characters is conveyed in minimalist,
even macho Hemingway-style prose. There is something
jarring and significant about this mismatch of style and

168

subject: even a tough young writer, with no use for extra adjectives and floral metaphors, chooses a passive voice for her characters.

Of course, Minot's are not the only anesthetized characters in contemporary fiction who are passive, numb, and basically detached — far from it. Depressed drifting was popularized in the late eighties by Jay McInerney's *Bright Lights, Big City,* with its apathetic, sometimes drug-dazed characters and its hazy-grasp-of-reality style. This kind of writing harkens back to the 1920s, with Jean Rhys's sad women sipping Pernod in Paris, wafting from unfortunate adventure to unfortunate adventure, but it has gained remarkable momentum in the past decade. Why do so many characters in popular, cutting-edge fiction seem to float passively through experience? It's always hard to analyze literary trends, to isolate the reasons people write the way they write, but that morning it was easy to imagine myself as a character in a story by Susan Minot on a mad, passive drift through life. It is precisely because the question of power is so pressing that the idea of giving it up is so fascinating. Drifting, giving up control, is a temporary imaginative salve for the unrelenting pressure to achieve. It's an appealing fantasy: passive and sensitive heroine buffeted by the harsh plot. It is the fantasy of control surrendered.

A French friend of mine insisted that only in this country is the issue of control so compelling. Americans are bent on regulating and controlling sexuality, he would say. France is freer, full of topless beaches and subway tunnels lined with ads showing more than an American amount of flesh. The French, he said, were less repressed and less obsessed with repression. Amid all of my friend's predictable bluster about American puritanism, he had an important point.

Catharine MacKinnon says don't read *Hustler* or fantasize about rape, and the handbooks say don't get too drunk or push too hard, don't tell her she has nice legs, and remember to use condoms. It is all part of the effort to regulate and control the way we think about sex, and that effort takes energy. It costs something. It's fueled by the vivid knowledge of what might happen if regulations were to fail. Along with the social efforts at control, the scrutiny of sexual behavior and thoughts, comes a barrage of images, colorful and richly distributed, of what happens if that control should break down.

I knew the rules, of course. I sometimes even followed the rules. But there is no denying that the stronger the rules, the stronger the fantasies of what lies outside of them. Powerful efforts to control sexual behavior create powerful images of control lost: beasts ravishing maidens in *Dracula,* snuff films in *Less Than Zero,* black-buckled bondage clothing in the fashion pages, the incest that is increasingly common in current fiction, and the list goes on.

It seemed to me, in the caffeinated drama of early dawn, that every moral parable, every sermon, had an image of hell, an image of what might happen but for the grace of God or man. The sometimes baroque, sometimes banal, sometimes cartoonlike, sometimes erotic images of violent sex show us fantasy unloosed; they show us the anatomy of danger, legs spread open for all to see.

Violent sex makes us want to buy more, read more, watch more, precisely because it dramatizes domination and submission. It strips the sometimes subtle struggle for power down to its bare essentials: who is on top, who is hurting whom, who is the victim. We are concerned with who is oppressed, sexually harassed, and raped, who pressures and pushes and makes advances, in the delicate tug-of-war of everyday social exchange. Maybe the more frequent public appearance of violent sex is a sign not of moral decay, of antifeminist gains, as some would have us believe, but rather a sign of the urge to resist sexual regulation from the right and from the left, and from the biological wild card of disease.

From Catharine MacKinnon to the protestors against the *Sports Illustrated* swimsuit issue to more mainstream theorists of sexual harassment, feminists are on the front lines of sexual regulation. Much of today's feminism in its most popular forms provides yet another source of repression, in the Freudian sense; feminism increasingly sides with "civilization," not its wild, edgy "discontents." Which is to say that feminism has come more and more to represent sexual thoughts and images censored, behavior checked, fantasies regulated. In my late-adolescent idiom, feminism was not about rebellion, but rules; it was not about setting loose, as it once was, it was about reining in.

As I looked out my window, at people in robes darting through the streets, grandmothers carrying flowers, I tried to picture the summer ahead. The plot came to me, strangely enough, in the voice of Susan Minot, Tama Janowitz, Jay McInerney, and others of their ilk: I move to a small walk-up in the East Village, with a bathtub in the kitchen. I get a job as a receptionist in a doctor's office and get picked up at a bar by a rich, older man who owns an art gallery and takes me to glamorous parties. He treats me like dirt. I stay with him, I don't know why. I curl up in bed at the end of the day. He calls, I go out with him again — what else is there to do?

The sound of the cars below broke my train of thought. I had caught myself in the middle of an unappealing fantasy of passivity: being carried along by fate, listening to the tarot cards, floating numb. What was I thinking? At the most uncharted moments in our lives we reach instinctively for the stock plots available to our generation, as trashy and clichéd as they may be. In the fifties it was love and marriage, or existentialism and Beat poetry in smoky bars. Now, if you're a woman, there's another role readily available: that of the sensitive female, pinched, leered at, assaulted daily by sexual advances, encroached upon, kept down, bruised by harsh reality. Among other things, feminism has given us this. A new stock plot, a new identity spinning not around love, not marriage, not communes, not materialism this time, but passivity and victimhood. This is not what I want, not even as a fantasy.

Afterword

Before everyone else was awake, my mother and I would go for walks on the beach. It was a time for us to talk, before buying the newspaper, making coffee, and beginning our day. This was one of those days when the fog was so thick you could barely see where you were going. We could hear the ocean, feel the salt against our face, but we couldn't see it.

In the middle of a long conversation about feminism, my mother suddenly asked if I ever thought about my high school graduation. Our class had been protesting the school's investment in companies that invested in South Africa. We wore black armbands around the lace or linen or silk of our white graduation dresses, and in the idleness of our second semester we had been holding sit-ins in the school lobby. Instead of the usual bland praise, our head-mistress delivered a fierce graduation speech about choosing the wrong enemies — the teachers and administrators of the school — out of excessive zeal. Standing in her long gray robe, her face white with anger, she warned us about the dangers of fighting your friends. Her speech was something of a scandal, her sharp words cutting into the blurry sentimentality of graduating, the pomp and circumstance. Sitting on the stage, we were captives, chastised and angry, and the audience of family and friends murmured and shifted in their seats.

Well, at least you've changed since then, my mother said, at least you've figured out that the battles are vaguer and more complicated than you'd imagined. We walked for a while without talking, the freezing waves catching our bare feet. I miss the clarity of high school sometimes, the white dresses, the black armbands, the underground paper, Xeroxed and distributed, filled with new outrage each month. As we walked back to the car, I confessed that I sometimes wished the world could be like Shakespeare, the way they teach it to you in seventh grade, with good and evil in opposition and patterns of imagery so clear that when the natural order is destroyed you know it because the horses are eating each other. The headmistress's speech has stayed with me all these years, and I know, as absurd as those black armbands may have been, that sometimes it is your friends you have to fight.

Notes

The Blue-Light System

1. Neil Gilbert, "Realities and Mythologies of Rape," *Society* 29 (May-June 1992); "Acquaintance Rape: 'Is Dating Dangerous?' " Rockville, Md.: American College Health Association, 1987; "HIV Infection and AIDS: What Everyone Should Know." ACHA, 1990; "What Are Sexually Transmitted Diseases?" Rockville, Md.: ACHA, 1989; "What You Should Know About Sexual Harassment." Princeton, N.J.: SHARE; " 'No' and Other Methods of Birth Control." Kenilworth, Ill.: Private Line, 1987; "Ten Ridiculous Ideas That Will Make a Mother Out of You." Oklahoma City: Planned Parenthood of Central Oklahoma, 1987; "Acquaintance Rape." Rockville, Md.: ACHA, 1992.
2. *Chronicle of Higher Education,* 15 May 1991.

Taking Back the Night

1. *Rag,* May 1991.
2. *Daily Princetonian,* 22 April 1988.
3. *Chronicle of Higher Education,* 17 December 1986.

4. *Nassau Weekly,* 23 April 1992.

5. *Rag,* May 1991; *Daily Princetonian,* 23 April 1991.

6. *Daily Princetonian,* 23 April 1991.

7. Ibid.

8. Ibid., 22 May 1991.

9. Ibid.

10. *New York Times,* 15 December 1991.

11. *Chronicle of Higher Education,* 19 December 1990.

12. Wendy Kaminer, *I'm Dysfunctional, You're Dysfunctional* (Reading, Mass.: Addison-Wesley, 1992), 33.

13. Betty Friedan, *The Second Stage* (New York: Summit Books, 1981), 362.

14. Andrea Dworkin, *Letters from a War Zone* (London: Secker and Warburg, 1988), 14.

15. *Daily Princetonian,.* 8 December 1981.

16. *Chronicle of Higher Education,* 15 May 1991.

17. Ibid., 19 June 1991.

18. Ibid., 27 May 1987.

The Rape Crisis, or "Is Dating Dangerous?"

1. *Ms.,* October 1985.

2. *New York Times,* 23 October 1985.

3. Neil Gilbert, "Realities and Mythologies of Rape," *Society* 29 (May-June 1992).

4. Ibid.

5. Ibid.

6. "Acquaintance Rape." Rockville, Md.: American College Health Association, 1992.

7. *New York Times,* 23 October 1985.

8. Naomi Wolf, *The Beauty Myth* (New York: William Morrow, 1991), 167.

9. Susan Brownmiller, *Against Our Will: Men, Women and Rape* (New York: Bantam, 1975), 5.

10. "Acquaintance Rape." Rockville, Md.: ACHA, 1992.

11. "Acquaintance Rape: Is Dating Dangerous?" Rockville, Md.: ACHA, 1987.

12. Susan Estrich, *Real Rape* (Cambridge: Harvard University Press, 1987), 102.

13. *Trenton Times,* 31 July 1992.

14. "Acquaintance Rape." Rockville, Md.: ACHA, 1992.

15. A Harvard date-rape task force came up with this definition of date rape: "Any act of sexual intercourse that occurs without the expressed consent of the person, or is accompanied by physical force or threat of bodily injury. Lack of consent may be indicated physically or verbally and needs only to be expressed once" (*Harvard Gazette,* 20 November 1992).

16. *New York,* 21 January 1991.

17. Elizabeth Fox-Genovese, *Feminism Without Illusions* (Chapel Hill: University of North Carolina Press, 1991), 21.

18. Robin Warshaw, *I Never Called It Rape* (New York: Harper and Row, 1988), 24.

19. Ibid., 174.

20. *Chronicle of Higher Education,* 26 March 1986.

21. Brownmiller, 189.

22. Andrea Parrot and Laurie Bechhofer, eds., *Acquaintance Rape: The Hidden Crime* (New York: John Wiley, 1991), 21.

23. "Acquaintance Rape: 'Is Dating Dangerous?' " Rockville, Md.: ACHA, 1991.

24. Mrs. John Farrar, *The Young Lady's Friend* (New York: Samuel S. and William Wood, 1857), 263.

25. Charlene L. Muelenhard and Jennifer L. Schrag, "Nonviolent Sexual Coercion," in Parrot and Bechhofer, 122.

26. Ibid., 123.

27. T. S. Arthur, *Advice to Young Ladies* (Boston: Phillips and Sampson, 1848), 151.

28. William Shakespeare (ed. Maurice Evans), *The Narrative Poems* (London: Penguin, 1989), 142.

29. Catharine MacKinnon, *Feminism Unmodified* (Cambridge: Harvard University Press, 1987), 82.

30. *Rag,* May 1991.

31. Ibid.

32. Inspector Thomas Byrnes, *Professional Criminals of America* (1886; reprint, New York: Chelsea House, 1969), 345.

33. Andrea Dworkin, *Letters from a War Zone* (London: Secker and Warburg, 1988), 14.

34. *New York Times,* 9 September 1992.

35. Billie Wright Dziech and Linda Weiner, *The Lecherous Professor: Sexual Harassment on Campus* (Chicago: University of Illinois Press, 1990), 53.

36. Susan Sontag, *Styles of Radical Will* (New York: Farrar, Straus and Giroux, 1976), 46.

37. "Acquaintance Rape." Rockville, Md.: ACHA, 1992.

38. Dziech and Weiner, 101.

39. Henry Fielding, *Tom Jones* (1749; reprint, London: Penguin, 1966), 471.

40. Catharine MacKinnon, *Toward a Feminist Theory of the State* (Cambridge: Harvard University Press, 1989), 146.

41. Gilbert, "Realities and Mythologies of Rape."

42. "Acquaintance Rape: 'Is Dating Dangerous?' " Rockville, Md.: ACHA, 1991.

43. Warshaw, 153.

44. Germaine Greer, *The Female Eunuch* (New York: McGraw-Hill, 1971), 59.

Reckless Eyeballing:
Sexual Harassment on Campus

1. "What You Should Know About Sexual Harassment." Princeton, N.J.: SHARE.

2. Ibid.

3. A standard definition given by a book about sexual harassment affirms that "harassment can also occur when no such formal [power] differential exists, if the behavior is unwanted by or offensive to the woman." Michele A. Paludi, ed., *Ivory Power: Sexual Harassment on Campus* (Albany: State University of New York Press, 1990), 38.

4. Catharine MacKinnon, *Feminism Unmodified* (Cambridge: Harvard University Press, 1987), 89.

5. *Chronicle of Higher Education,* 24 April 1991.

6. Billie Wright Dziech and Linda Weiner, *The Lecherous Professor: Sexual Harassment on Campus* (Chicago: University of Illinois Press, 1990), 180.

7. Sue Rosenberg Zalk, "Men in the Academy," in Paludi, 143.

8. Dziech and Weiner, 180.

9. Paludi, 122.

10. "Sexual Harassment: A Hidden Issue." Washington, D.C.: Project on the Status and Education of Women, 1978.

11. *Chronicle of Higher Education,* 10 July 1991.

12. "Due Process in Sexual Harassment Complaints," *Academe* 77 (September-October 1991).

13. Dziech and Weiner, 49.

14. *New York Times,* 3 May 1992.

15. MacKinnon, *Toward a Feminist Theory of the State* (Cambridge: Harvard University Press, 1989), 127.

16. Louise Fitzgerald and Lauren Weitzman, "Men Who Harass: Speculation and Data," in Paludi, 139.

17. Princeton, N.J.: SHARE.

18. "Acquaintance Rape." Rockville, Md.: ACHA, 1992.

19. MacKinnon, *Toward a Feminist Theory of the State*, 149.

20. Jacquelyn Dowd Hall, " 'The Mind That Burns in Each Body': Women, Rape and Racial Violence," in Christine Stansell, Ann Snitow, and Sharon Thompson, eds., *Powers of Desire: The Politics of Sexuality* (New York: Monthly Review Press, 1983), 329.

21. Princeton, N.J.: SHARE.

22. Ibid.

23. Kathryn Quina, "The Victimizations of Women," in Paludi, ed., 99.

24. *New York*, 16 November 1992.

25. Ibid.

26. Joan Didion, *The White Album* (New York: Farrar, Straus and Giroux, 1979), 116.

27. Mary Koss, "Changed Lives: The Psychological Impact of Sexual Harassment," in Paludi, ed., 73.

CATHARINE MACKINNON, THE ANTIPORN STAR

1. Catharine MacKinnon, *Feminism Unmodified* (Cambridge: Harvard University Press, 1987), 171.

2. Ibid., 155.

3. Vladimir Nabokov, *The Annotated Lolita* (New York: Vintage Books, 1991), 314.

4. MacKinnon, *Feminism Unmodified*, 181.

5. Wendy Kaminer, "Feminists Against the First Amendment," *Atlantic Monthly*, November 1992.

6. *New York Times Magazine*, 6 October 1991.

7. Susan Sontag, *Styles of Radical Will* (New York: Farrar, Straus and Giroux, 1969), 66.

8. Ibid.

754323

GAYLORD R